A WOMAN WHO LAUGHED

A WOMAN WHO LAUGHED

Henrietta Soltau
who laughed at impossibilities
and cried: 'It shall be done'

MILDRED CABLE
FRANCESCA FRENCH

PRISCA

Pickering & Inglis

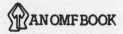 AN OMF BOOK

Copyright © 1934
Mildred Cable and Francesca French

First paperback edition published 1984
by Pickering & Inglis,
3 Beggarwood Lane,
Basingstoke, Hants RG23 7LP,
United Kingdom

First published in hardback 1934 by
The China Inland Mission, London.

ISBN 0 7208 0568 6

Printed and bound in Great Britain by
Hunt Barnard Printing Ltd., Aylesbury, Bucks.

CONTENTS

Introduction to *PRISCA*   10

Prologue to the first Edition   13

Foreword to the *PRISCA* Edition   14

The Dew of Dawn   17

The Wings of the Morning   67

The Heat of the Day   141

Steady Until the Going Down of the Sun   227

Epilogue   240

INTRODUCTION TO *PRISCA*

We live in an age of increasing perplexity for the Christian woman. The Women's Liberation Movement itself is varying in its mood, swinging from extreme stridency, to an anxiety that perhaps it has gone too far and that women are actually losing out as a result. The Christian Church, on the other hand, is also uncertain in its approach, and this is true not only in the wider ecumenical context, but in evangelical circles also. These can show deeply different attitudes. An article was published in a leading evangelical magazine which maintained that to forbid a woman to preach was unscriptural and un-Christlike, whereas a sermon in a New York church taught that a woman should never be allowed to handle her own money, but should hand it over to her husband because he was her head.

In the light of this it is obviously important for Christian women not to be cowed by these conflicting pressures, but to think their whole position through, honestly and biblically. I believe that a good way of doing that is for women to discuss these things together, and of course one of the best means for this is the reading of books.

In the secular world, many women's presses have sprung to life, again reflecting the various organisations from which they have come. One of these is the *Virago Press*, whose object is to provide an outlet to the writings of women both past and present, and to cover a wide range of subjects (judicious selection is called for on the part of the reader!).

It is my hope that the PRISCA series can achieve a similar aim, and that it should be an imprint which will publish books by or about Christian women. I would not want it to be felt however, that all PRISCA books must be about specifically 'women's' subjects — home-maker or career woman, bringing up children, etc. - though these may well be covered. Neither, let me hasten to add, is this a kind of 'Christian Women's Lib' series! The name 'PRISCA' was chosen because the New Testament Priscilla illustrates best how the women in the Bible lived full and varied lives. She seems to have combined technical skills, hospitality, doctrinal clarity and counselling wisdom, and all this with the obvious love and respect of the Apostle Paul. We do not need Women's Lib to tell us that women have always made a big contribution to society and to the life of God's people, a contribution which, we hope, will be highlighted by this series.

What I really want, therefore, is for the PRISCA series to be an outlet for women to write books about anything that interests them, whether it involves their own lives, their thinking, other people or the world around them — anything in fact that inspires them to put pen to paper! It will be good, therefore, if this series encourages new writers as well as those who have already been published, while we hope also to republish some of the 'Golden Oldies' of the past.

The Christian Church has had its Freya Starks too,

women who have travelled and adventured for the Gospel; while other women wrote books which have long been out of print and forgotten, and such works may be of great value to us today.

Above all it is my desire that God may be glorified in such a series, and that we Christian women may be encouraged as we strive to fill our God-given place in society, to use our talents, and to 'adorn the doctrine' of our Saviour in everything.

Elizabeth Catherwood

PROLOGUE

The writing of this memoir has been an expression of love, made possible by the intimacy which existed between Henrietta Soltau and the two writers. From December 1843, when she was born, to February 1934, when she died, world events moved rapidly and social conditions changed drastically. Were it not for the long hours of conversation, when the past lived again for her, and through her for her listeners, this story could not have been told.

Fourteen years ago, when Miss Soltau was on the point of destroying all her accumulation of papers, letters and diaries, Jessie Gregg, her dearly-loved daughter in the faith, intervened and persuaded her to spare, for the benefit of a coming generation, these records of God's leading and provision. When she was convinced that she had one final witness to bear, Henrietta Soltau took the whole bundle and gave it over to the charge of Mildred Cable to be dealt with at her discretion; it being tacitly understood that the subject would never again be mentioned between them. Her confidence was respected, and not until she died were the papers produced.

Let those who would know the beauty and dignity of a guided life read this volume to their profit and instruction.

MC & FF, 1934

FOREWORD TO
THE *PRISCA* EDITION

Mildred Cable and Francesca French published this
biography of Henrietta Soltau in June 1934, four months
after her death. To mark the fiftieth anniversary of both
these events, we in the *PRISCA PRESS* are now republishing
the book as the first of our 'Golden Oldies'.

There are several reasons for this. First and foremost,
I always feel that reading the lives of God's people is
one of the richest ways of encouraging our own Christian
faith. We know, for example, that it is an unchanging
biblical promise that God will supply all our needs, but
such a promise is wonderfully underlined by the many
ways in which God proved this in Henrietta Soltau's life.
We can learn from her faults and failures, her wisdom
and her kindness, and, above all, from her unfailing
evangelistic zeal. The practical side of her nature, too,
is worth noting, whether shown by her careful
housekeeping or by her quickness in locking the outside
doors, so that the guests at a down-and-outs' party could
not get out of the hall until they had heard the Gospel!
Hebrews 11 has been called the 'picture gallery of faith'.
Henrietta Soltau's portrait is one of the twentieth
century's most attractive acquisitions.

Then, secondly, I have been struck by the way in
which her life and the problems which she faced are so
relevant to those of many christian women today. How,

for example, should she assert her own independence of thought and life against an upbringing which, though very loving, had been somewhat narrow and circumscribing? Then again, should she, a woman, preach the Gospel to men? Many thought not, and yet she saw many conversions when she did so. Long before Evangelism Explosion was dreamed of, she was taking the Gospel to everyone in her village, using every stratagem that she could, so that 'by all means she might save some'. She also dealt with the agonising, complex question of how best to help missionaries' children, and she also saw the tragedies which can arise on the mission field as a result of unhappy personal relationships among the workers. Most of all, perhaps, in an age like ours which has seen a flowering of the Charismatic movement, it is deeply moving to read of a woman who in 1882 so experienced the power and blessing of the Holy Spirit that she could say, 'Although I have been converted for years, I never knew such joy as I have experienced today'.

Thirdly, Mildred Cable and Francesca French themselves are writers who through their lives and writing were greatly used of God, and I hope that we shall be reading more of them in the *PRISCA PRESS*. I know that their desire would be that through this book of theirs, Henrietta Soltau, woman of God, though she is dead, should yet speak to us today, supremely of the Saviour whom she loved and served.

E.C.

THE DEW OF DAWN

I

THE child Henrietta Eliza Soltau was born into a good man's household in Plymouth on the 8th of December in the year of grace 1843. The family inheritance was one of great moral rectitude. Her grandfather was a godly man and had exerted strong philanthropic influence in that city. He was prominent in good works, and notably was one of the founders of the Plymouth Free School, in which the scholars, though trained in the knowledge of the Scriptures, were under no compulsion to attend the Scripture lesson should this be in opposition to the wishes of the parents. Under such intelligent guidance the school grew to be one of the largest in England. His own views on social matters were of so austere and puritanical an order that, as member of the Town Council, he even opposed the construction of a theatre. He died at a comparatively early age, leaving a widow and six children, the second of whom was Henry William, father of Henrietta.

Henry William Soltau was given all the educational advantages possible to a young man of his day. After taking his degree at Trinity College, Cambridge, he proceeded to study law, and in

due time was called to the Chancery Bar. His
portrait shows him as a man of handsome and
distinguished bearing, purposeful, upright, and of
more than the ordinary mental acumen—a type
combining moral and intellectual qualities of an
unusually high order.

His thoroughness was evidenced by the fact
that he studied Hebrew in order to better understand the Old Testament, and the keenness of
his critical faculty was shown by his declaration,
in later years, that, as a young man, earnestly
seeking after Truth and with opportunities to
listen to the leading Evangelical teachers, he
could never remember hearing what he styled a
'clear Gospel' preached. The fundamental distinction between salvation as a gift of God in
response to faith, and salvation as the reward
of good works, had never, in his opinion, been
made sufficiently clear, even by those prominent
preachers and theologians. So logical a mind as
that of Henry Soltau was dissatisfied so long as
any possible ambiguity remained to confuse the
vital issue.

After completing his studies he settled in London,
and became the popular member of a social circle
in which his musical, intellectual and literary
attainments were greatly appreciated. Town life
satisfied one side of his nature, and the years passed
quickly, filled as they were with a diversity of

interests and attended by sufficient success to satisfy professional ambitions.

When he was thirty-two years of age the shadow of a great sorrow fell across his path, for he was summoned to his mother's bedside by the news of her serious illness. The long coach journey from London to Plymouth seemed endless to the anxious son, especially as the dragging hours brought a conviction that he would not see his mother alive. As the coach rolled on toward the west country he sat and reviewed his life for the past years, till he seemed to himself as one summoned unawares to the bar of judgment, where he must face the realities of life, of death, and the demands of his God.

A few hours later he was standing by the coffin in which his mother's body had been laid. The fundamental sincerity of the young man found expression in the brief petition: "Lord, if Thou dost not save me I am lost for ever!" His eyes were immediately opened to the knowledge which man's words seemed hitherto only to have veiled. He understood grace and accepted salvation, full, free and triumphant.

A young man could scarcely be faced with a situation making greater demands on moral force than was Henry Soltau on his return to London. His old friends were there, expecting him to join, as before, in their social pastimes. Though they could not fail to immediately notice a change in him, yet it was unthinkable to them that Henry Soltau should have become so fanatical a Christian as to cease to be good company. It was then that he faced his personal problem. Should he conform sufficiently to the ways of his former life to enable him to retain his place in the social circle, and possibly win some in it to Christ? Should he make it his life-work to reach those from whom his training and culture forced recognition and ensured a hearing? Or must he view these things as ' treasures of Egypt,' unworthy to be compared with the riches of the reproach of Christ, abandon them wholly, and follow Him 'without the camp'?

He looked on the Church of England to which, by upbringing, he belonged. At that period it was largely sunk in lethargy and worldly concern. If this new life were to be sustained, it must find some channel through which nourishment would come, and also an outlet through which the force within would reach the need without, and realizing that the Church would fail him on both issues, he left it.

Henry Soltau's moral nature was of a temper which never admitted a shadow of compromise. For him compromise was virtual death, the pact between cowardice and comfort, masquerading under the title of expediency. Thanks to the stand he took, a very brief time sufficed to alienate his worldly friends, and that more by their initiative than his own. He even felt compelled to give up his practice at the Bar, and retire to Plymouth.

The attraction offered by that city was the presence there of a remarkable group of men who were, at this time, making a contribution of incalculable value to the whole Church of Christ. Here was a congenial circle of friends composed of men in no respect inferior in mental equipment to those from which he had just withdrawn. He found in it scholars, writers, artists, orators, men of analytical genius and scientists, each of whom had broken with the Church of England or some Nonconformist body, to join fellowship with a company who were popularly called ' The Plymouth Brethren.'

These men were dominated by a passion for reality in spiritual things. Having recognized that God *is* they could not admit of any manner of life in which He was not pre-eminent. That pre-eminence once admitted, no life could be considered save one wholly controlled by His laws. Yet ever conscious of failure to fulfil the demands of law, there was but one way of escape— the Divinely appointed sacrifice for sin, and on this they staked their all.

They studied the Scriptures with the intense concentration that the scientist gives to his study of natural phenomena, and the Church is debtor to this hour to the men who were brave enough to divest themselves of the cerements of preconceived notions and ready-made truth, and whose passionate devotion was rewarded by spiritual revelation. Study of the Scriptures, and propagation of the Gospel, were now to Henry Soltau the first business of life.

Far away in Yorkshire lived a county family of the name of Tate. It was a wealthy, influential clan whose children were brought up to enjoy fashionable life in accordance with their station. One of the daughters, however, refused to bow to family views on matrimony, and, taking the law into her own hands, she married the man of her choice. Her husband did not live for many years and she was left a young widow with two children. Her father's home became a natural shelter to her for the few remaining years of her own life, and there she brought up her son and daughter.

The girl, Lucy, when left an orphan was cared for by two ladies who acted as guardians to her. They loved travel and life on the Continent, and she spent much time with them in Italy, but when they wintered in England it was generally in Plymouth, where they had many friends and where they could enjoy the gaieties of a fashionable set.

One year they arrived there as usual by boat from Naples, and went direct to the hotel where they generally stayed. Their first enquiry was about the social season, whether many of their friends were staying in the town and if many balls were taking place.

"Balls, ladies!" exclaimed the hotel-keeper. "Why, Plymouth has gone mad since you were last here."

"What do you mean?" they asked.

"I mean what I say, ladies. There are no balls in the town this year, and everyone is given up to religious gatherings. Plymouth has just gone mad with religion. The preachers have taken the big concert hall, and every night you have to be there an hour ahead if you want a seat."

"Do you mean to say that the kind of people *we* know are attending revival meetings in the theatre?"

"That is just what they are doing, ladies, and they are getting converted one by one."

Full of excitement at the prospect of a new experience, Lucy persuaded her chaperones to come that very evening to the hall where the meetings were held. They found a big crowd, which listened with rapt attention to the speakers who addressed them from the stage. These preachers formed a striking group, whose chief characteristic was its intense earnestness. It was impossible to remain frivolous under their solemn appeal, and everywhere among the audience signs of spiritual distress broke out, while many wept, sobbed and cried to God for mercy.

The three ladies returned to their hotel shaken by all they had seen, and deeply stirred by what they had heard. Next night, and the next again, they were back at the meeting, and soon all three of them were converted.

Lucy, in her new-born joy, could not rest for thinking of an aged kinswoman, away in Yorkshire. This relative was eighty years of age, and if she did not soon hear the wonderful tidings of salvation it might be too late for Lucy to tell her. Without delay the girl bought a place on the Yorkshire coach and started off from Plymouth on her urgent errand.

As soon as greetings had been exchanged, the young girl sat down by the old lady and spoke to her of the matter which was in her heart.

"Aunt," she said, "I have found out how sin is forgiven, and I came here on purpose to tell you."

To her amazement the old lady answered:

"My dear, I have wanted to know this very thing for years past."

If the old lady was keen on spiritual things, other members of the household were equally determined that Lucy should not be allowed to upset her with religious talk. They chatted, introduced various topics and brought the unwelcome conversation to a close. At dinner, however, the aunt demanded that Lucy be put to sit by her, and presently she whispered:

"Come and sleep with me to-night, my dear, and tell me all you can about the forgiveness of sin."

That night the old lady found Christ. Next day she told her doctor and from one to another the good news spread until the whole neighbourhood was quickened with spiritual interest.

Lucy knew that Plymouth was the town where she would find the Bible-teaching her soul longed for, and, the object of her visit to Yorkshire having been attained, she took the long journey back to Devonshire. Here, before long, she met Henry William Soltau, they were mutually attracted, and in 1841 she became his wife.

The first eight years of their married life were spent at Plymouth, during which period six children were born to them:

Lucy Elizabeth
Henrietta Eliza
Dorothea Agnes (afterwards Mrs. R. Hill)
Elizabeth Maria
George
Mary Amelia (afterwards Mrs. Gribble).

Later they moved to Exmouth where two more children were born :

Henry
Charlotte Matilda (afterwards Mrs. Warren).

In Northam House, near Bideford, William, their ninth and last child, was born.

During the years of residence in Plymouth, widely divergent theological views came to be held by different members of the local meeting, which resulted in so serious a division that the Assembly was divided into two branches, which were never again united. Subsequent to J. N. Darby's visit in 1845, a secession took place in which Darby withdrew from the large meeting, which numbered as many as a thousand adherents and was under the leadership of B. W. Newton. Darby started an independent company of worshippers ; but divisions rapidly multiplied, as was inevitable when a group of such strong and subtle-minded men began to dogmatize upon the various aspects of Christian truth, and to attempt the elucidation of mysteries which baffle human thought.

These sad days of division caused so much distress to Mr. and Mrs. Soltau that they thought best to leave Plymouth for Exmouth, where they spent three years, and at the close of this period moved on to the village of Northam near Bideford, where ten happy, useful years were spent.

During the whole of this time Mr. Soltau travelled extensively, speaking at large meetings throughout the United Kingdom. The tender and sympathetic nature which made him a popular member of every circle had been deepened by years of faithful Christian service, and his gift of insight into human nature taught him where to be stern and where gentle.

The perpetual recurrence of dissension among members of the various meetings made severe demands on time and strength, and only those of his intimate circle appreciated the cost to himself of these unseemly quarrels. The judicial qualities which would certainly have brought him into prominence had he pursued his career at the Bar, were constantly called into service, not so much for counsel on legitimate matters of spiritual import, as in regard to arbitration on contentious disputes regarding details of theological minutiæ.

In 1861 the family moved to Exeter, where Mr. Soltau devoted a large portion of his time to the writing of books, through which his name became widely known. His volume on the Tabernacle is a work of patient research, and still holds its place as a standard book of reference on that subject. In 1867 he paid a short visit to London, where he spoke six times on one Sunday, some of the meetings being in the open-air. The abnormal effort proved too great, and shortly after he suffered a stroke of paralysis, which prevented him from ever being able to speak again in public.

In 1870, knowing his years to be drawing to a close, he moved to Barnstaple that he might end his earthly life near his beloved friend, Mr. Robert Chapman. In 1873 his eldest daughter died, and from this shock he never recovered. He lived on for two years and four months, but during the whole period he never left his room. On July 1, 1875, he died.

The testimony of one of his sons is as follows :

" His life was one of great simplicity and unyielding uprightness. His one desire was to exalt the Name of the Lord Jesus and to serve Him in serving His people. He never looked back, he had counted the cost and kept his eye fixed on the goal. He had the joy of seeing all his nine children early converted, and, as they grew up, giving themselves to the Lord's service. He was a wise and tender father, and the home was a centre of love and happiness. What he taught in public he ever sought to practise in the home, and he was fond of dwelling on the Divine order of responsibility : 'First yourself, then the home, then the Church, then the world.' "

II

HENRIETTA ELIZA was the second child of Henry and Lucy Soltau. One of her earliest recollections was that of seeing her father working at his easel on those diagrams of the Tabernacle which are so intimately associated with his name. Another was that of standing with him at an open-air meeting, at the close of which she had to seek the support of his trousered leg, to which she clung, as a shower of cabbage stalks and rotten eggs fell around them. He also spent long hours with the microscope, engaged on botanical studies, and some of his slides find a place to-day in the British Museum.

The religious convictions held by her parents precluded any free social intercourse with those whose theological views differed from their own. Moreover, the stigma of Brethrenism was upon them, and county society could not smile upon such a violation of the social code as was involved by street preaching and reference to the " things of God " in season and out of season. The result of these restrictions was that the family circle became the children's world.

The dearest friends of those childish days were William and Sally Challice. They were old and faithful servants in the Soltau family, to whom they were attached by a peculiar bond of love and gratitude.

Here is the story as told by Henrietta : " One day my grandfather was walking on the beach at Teignmouth and saw a poor little boy sobbing most bitterly as if his heart would break. He went over to him and found that he wore workhouse clothes.

" ' What is the matter, my child ? ' he asked.

" ' Please, sir, I belong to the Workhouse and I have run away because they beat me.'

" The boy showed my grandfather the marks on his arms and back where he was beaten and, ' Please, sir,' he said, ' I will never go back there again.'

" My grandfather took the matter in hand and arranged to rescue the boy. When he knew that something would be done for him, William said :

" ' Please, sir, get Sally also, she is my only sister.'

" So my kind grandfather took both the children and trained them for servants in his house. They were devoted to him and to my grandmother.

" When they were old, my aunts provided a nice cottage home for them where we loved to stay as their guests."

The atmosphere of the home induced mental maturity, as the most serious subjects were constantly under discussion, and no frivolity found a place in the conversation. Even to be born and brought up among the Brethren of that day was in itself a moral suasion, yet unconsciously, but inevitably, these parents brought to bear on every matter of daily life a breadth of outlook which was the result of the years they had spent in 'the world.' Religious views might cause them to deny their children the advantage of association with companions of their own age and social standing, who were disapproved of as 'worldly,' but they could not prevent the strong influence which emanated from themselves, and which was the direct result of their early social life, of college contacts, and of association with men and women of a wide circle. These were of inestimable benefit to themselves and their children, though they would have been loath to acknowledge that any value attached to association with 'the world.'

Every evening found the family assembled around the long dining-table, the girls doing needlework of the most utilitarian order, and the mother reading aloud some serious book. No fiction of any kind was ever allowed in the house, and imagination had to feed on such works as *The Story of the Persecution of the Albigenses, Port Royal des Champs,* and like records of persecution and martyrdom.

Daily attendance at an excellent country school called Tusculum, whose head master was a leading light in Brethrenism, limited the range of educational advantage to be enjoyed by the boys. The girls had a resident governess, but all owed much to the habit of reading good books aloud with their intelligent parents. Henrietta could never even learn to play the piano because her hands were crippled with chilblains for months each year. As a result of such meagre education the boys, in later years, often found themselves inadequately equipped for the requirements of the very work to which their father had so sincerely dedicated them. The best scholarship which England of that period could supply, had enabled him to bring the powers of a highly cultured intellect to bear on the study of the Scriptures, but this legitimate inheritance he denied to his own sons, and in later years incurred the censure of their maturer judgment.

In religious matters the teaching they received was absolutely dogmatic. Each child was pronounced to be in a state of alienation from God until the decisive hour when, through an act of faith, salvation was appropriated. There was no borderland, just one clear-cut line between life and death, and each individual they met stood on one or other side of that line. Henrietta reached the age of eleven without having made the momentous decision. She was keenly aware of her unregenerate state, and all the conversation to which she listened would come back to her in the lonely hours of the night, when she sometimes lay in an agony of fear lest she might die before morning and fall into the hands of that God whose judgments she had been taught so to fear.

An indelible impression was made upon her sensitive mind by a letter which her mother received, telling of the death of a little child, ten years old, from scarlet fever. This child had ' come to Christ and given sweet testimony.' The letter was read to the elder children in the hope that it might rouse in them a sense of the danger of procrastination in the matter of conversion. Coincident with this, several of the family, including Henrietta, were taken ill with measles, and for a time the baby's life was in danger. The realization of death being forcibly thrust on her mind, set Henrietta in an agony of fear.

When night came she was seized with the old terror that she might not live till morning, and she cried to God to blot out her sins, promising amendment if her life might be spared. Her parents attributed her tears to physical pain, and failed to understand that the thought uppermost in the mind of their sensitive child was, " What if I die like that little girl ? " As she recovered human nature reasserted itself, and she almost repented her rash promise to be good. The whole incident left her irritable, unhappy and restless, but each night fears stalked afresh, and the little child would hide under the bedclothes suffering the pangs of 'conviction of sin,' the need of which always found its place in the Lord's Day exhortation.

On the night of February 22, 1854, she so feared to sleep lest she should die unsaved before the kindly sun should rise and restore her sense of confidence, that she heard the clock strike hour after hour. At last she slept and dreamed: "I was in a dreary place alone. I could not tell where I was or find my way home, so I sat down and cried. Presently a stranger drew near with a very kind face, and said:

"'Little girl, what is the matter? Take my hand and I will lead you.'

"I sprang up and took his hand, feeling that I could trust that kind face. He led me out of the barren marsh into a lovely wood filled with moss and flowers, and I asked if I might always stay in this lovely place.

"'No,' he said, 'we must go on further.'

"We came out of the wood by a steep hill, and walked over a narrow pathway with a precipice on either side. I skipped along refusing to take the hand he held out to me, until I nearly slipped over the edge, when he caught and held me in his strong grasp. The hills seemed to be slippery and the way difficult, so I clung to my Guide, who spoke cheering words.

" When we reached the top I saw the beautiful Heavenly City ahead, with pearly gates and streets of gold, and white-robed multitudes playing harps, who filled the air with lovely music. As I ran to the open gateway desiring to enter, I saw One coming to meet me who was so beautiful that I knew it must be the Lord Jesus, and I saw His pierced Hands which He held out to me. . . . I awoke, the night was dark and I was alone and trembling all over. I burst into tears, saying :

" ' I can never enter there, for I have no white robe. I am not saved. What shall I do ? I am full of sin.'

" Then I heard His voice saying to me : ' Come unto Me, all ye that labour and are heavy laden, and I will give you rest,' and I cried out :

" ' Lord, I come to Thee. Wash me and save me.'

" In a moment the light broke on me, I knew that I was His for ever, and my heart was full of joy."

In her dream, man's distorted representation of God faded from her mind, and instead she saw a Saviour whose presence satisfied her every childish longing. The vision of Christ which remained with her through life was that of a beautiful figure welcoming her in the setting of a pearly gate, surrounded by white-robed multitudes, to the sound of exquisite music.

Her first act on waking in the morning was to call her sister Agnes into her bed and tell her she had been saved in the night, whereupon Agnes cried and said she too wanted to be saved. When their mother came into the room to call them to dress, they threw their arms around her and told her that both had passed from death unto life, and as she wept for joy they rushed on to announce the good news to their father. . . .

On the first of August, 1854, in the very early morning, a little group gathered on the banks of the river Torridge, when Mrs. Soltau, her sister-in-law, and her three little girls aged respectively ten, eleven and twelve, along with the gardener, passed through the waters of baptism. Mr. Robert Chapman performed the rite, and later all adjourned to a neighbouring house where they celebrated the ordinance of the Lord's Supper.

Mrs. Soltau was a strong-minded woman who sometimes incurred the disapprobation of the local assembly. As a girl her dress had been too fashionable but, in time, the bonnet trimmed with a spray of pink roses was abandoned, even the beloved guitar was laid aside, and all her jewellery went into George Müller's hands to help feed his orphan family. She had, however, resolutely refused to accept immersion, and this point she never yielded until she shared the rite with the first of her own children.

Robert Chapman, who baptized Henrietta Soltau, was another of the men who renounced all prospects of a worldly career in order to give himself wholly to the service of Christ, and who found his congenial sphere among the Brethren. Son of Sir George Chapman, his youth was spent in courtly circles, but he severed himself from these things that he might obtain the coveted privilege of being a preacher of the Gospel. He lived in a cottage at Barnstaple, but many found him out there, and men of various nationalities were guests at the humble board, where the master of the house blacked his visitors' boots, but could speak nobly and wisely to them in seven different languages. The children all loved him for his serious interest in their doings and also for the beauty of his courtesy. He would rise and hold the door open for Ettie or Agnes as deferentially as he did it for their mother.

He was the first friend to whom the children confided the news of their conversion, and he listened to their story with grave sympathy. Then turning to Henrietta he asked her, very seriously, if she could ever doubt again that she belonged to Christ.

" Oh, no, of course not," was her instant reply.

" Children," he said, " some day, it may be years ahead, the great enemy Satan will certainly try and make you doubt the love of Christ, but remember, 'No man shall pluck you out of His Hand.' If doubt comes it will be from Satan, not from God.

"Never forget," he continued, "how blessed it is to have the heart stored with the Word of God. Before I was brought to the Lord I slept with my copy of Homer under my pillow, but in the year 1823 the Lord brought me to Himself and gave me also a vision, the only vision in my life. I distinctly saw an arm and a hand pointing with a finger to an open Bible and I believe the Bible was open at Psalm 119. Ever since, this has been my meat and drink."

III

CONVERSION, as understood by these earnest people, had not fulfilled its end when the individual passed from death to life. From that hour serious responsibility must be assumed, and even these children were to reckon themselves debtors to all men. From the age of eleven Henrietta and her sister Lucy were given Sunday School classes, consisting of half a dozen little children from four to six years old. They proved a great delight to the two girls, especially as attendance at Sunday School included the pleasure of a picnic lunch, carried in a basket and eaten in the schoolroom, and, as soon as this was disposed of, the visiting of their small flock before afternoon session. "By this means we learned our first lessons of poverty, suffering and need."

On weekdays they often joined the pupils of Mrs. Hake's school for walks, and one of their companions on these sea-shore excursions was little Edmund Gosse, a child of precocious scientific attainments under whose tuition they learnt to observe the habits of the little creatures which lived in the pools and among the rocks of that fascinating Devonshire coast. Little Edmund was highly trained by his father, the famous naturalist, and nothing escaped his microscopic eyes.

On the religious side the children just as surely imitated their parents, and Henrietta says, " Down by the sea, on the sand-hills and among the rocks, we held our little prayer-meetings." One who took part in these excursions tells that " Ettie was known in these days as ' Little Evangelist.' The first time I saw her she was eleven years old, and I was eight. In a most winning way she put her arms round me, kissed me and said, ' Do you love Jesus ? ' "

The next move was to a country house called Durrant which stood between Bideford and Northam. " It was a large old rambling house," writes Miss Soltau, " with shrubberies and two walled gardens, a long carriage drive, fine old ilex trees and many flowering shrubs, each side of the drive, white and pink May trees, laburnum and chestnut alternately. We had a donkey and a small cart so that we could get more easily to the sea." Here life was more circumscribed even than in Barnstaple, and several quiet years were spent in the peaceful atmosphere of the family circle.

One of their neighbours was a man who kept race-horses. The children loved to watch the horses being exercised, and before long they were on friendly terms with some of the stable-boys.

The greatest treat was when a groom would lift
them into the saddle and let them ride the lovely
creatures. Before long the boys used to run freely
in and out of the stables, and Ettie followed her
brothers. Mr. Soltau would not forbid it, realizing
that this was the only access to an otherwise
unapproachable house, but he took " Little Evangelist " on his knee and spoke seriously to her.

" Ettie, my dear, when you go to the stables
always take one of the papers from that shelf
and give it to the boy you talk with," and this she
did.

It was a godless household. Its master had no
use for religion, but the prayers of the Soltaus and
Ettie's charming ways secured the acceptance of
a Bible by one of the stable-boys.

One day the rich man was taken ill and a week
later the whole village knew that he was dying.
Among the Christian community earnest and
believing prayer was offered on his behalf, yet, a
few days later, when the funeral procession passed
Durrant House, no one knew if any instinct toward repentance had been awakened in that hard
heart and Ettie truly voiced the thought of her
elders when she said :

" I wonder why God did not hear prayer."

Immediately after the funeral the servants were
dismissed, the large establishment was scattered and
the house abandoned.

Many years later William Soltau was preaching in the open air. At the close of the meeting a horsy-looking man came up and touched his cap :

" Be you Mr. George, Mr. Henry or Mr. William, sir ? "

" My name is William," was the answer, " but I don't know what yours is."

The man grinned. " When you was a little boy, sir, I often gave you a ride on my 'oss. Where is Miss Ettie ? I want you to tell her about that there Bible that she gave me. When Master was taken so bad and the doctor said he couldn't live, he was in a terrible fright and called out on God for mercy.

" ' Bring me a Bible,' he shouted.

" They that was looking after him tried to pacify him and said there warn't such a thing in the 'ouse.

" ' Then find me one,' he yelled, ' and bring it quick or it'll be too late.'

" I were the only chap in the place as 'ad a Bible, and that was the one Miss Ettie give me, and I 'ad it 'id away in my box, fear anyone should see it, but when my old master called out that way, I ran and fetched it out and brought it to 'is door. They took it in and read it to 'im and after that 'e was real quiet and died peaceful like.

" Tell Miss Ettie, sir, that after that I gave my heart to Christ : I often think of her and the way she used to speak to us stable-boys."

IV

MR. SOLTAU was often away from home, visiting Brethren Assemblies and holding Missions, while the mother's hands were full with the claims of her young family. An impending tragedy had already thrown a shadow over Henry Soltau; for several years he had suffered from trouble in his eyes, and suddenly, one day, he became totally blind. Notwithstanding this trial his strong religious convictions overcame physical disability, and he carried on evangelistic work in spite of it. It now became the elder girls' main work to lead their father about, take him to all his nearer preaching engagements, and to spend many hours each day reading aloud to him the theological, historic and scientific works that he wished to hear.

In 1861 the family moved to Exeter, and the two elder girls went ahead to get the house ready. As soon as it was known that two daughters of the renowned Henry Soltau were in the town, and that they were there to make ready for their parents, they were surrounded by old friends of their father's. One of the first to arrive was George Brealey, an evangelist of great native capacity but humble origin, an earnest but rough-and-ready man. He greeted them in his brusque way.

" Well, you young ladies, I hope you love the Lord and I hope you have come to work for Him."

Their answer could leave him in no doubt as to their earnestness, but they confided to him that, being strangers in the place, they did not know how or where to begin, the more so as they felt quite unaccustomed to town life.

George Brealey became closely associated with the Soltau family during the time they lived in Exeter. He was a lamplighter and a shoemaker but, had he been questioned on the subject, he would have declared, as did another great man who once plied that same humble trade : " Sir, my business is the extension of Christ's Kingdom, and I only make shoes to pay expenses." The scholar Soltau and the craftsman Brealey tramped the streets of Exeter and the neighbouring villages together, proclaiming Christ at every street corner. One winter they preached in every public house of the town. Having spent his own youth in riotous living, fighting and gambling, Brealey had a message for such men and was tireless in seeking to win them to the Saviour.

In Henrietta and Lucy Soltau he detected kindred spirits, and zeal enough to attack a terrible quarter known as Newtown where the people were heathen and the children could only be described as little demons. Before many weeks had passed this energetic man had secured an old carpenter's shop which, in his capable hands, was rapidly made sufficiently habitable to be used for a Sunday School and for evangelistic meetings.

This building was soon overcrowded, and other premises hired which, though larger, were old and rickety. These were used for two years, but then became too dangerous. It was a motley crowd which assembled there week by week. Most of the Sunday School scholars came from the brickfields, and were far too wild and unruly to be welcomed in any more conventional gathering. Dirty faces, ragged clothes and hair matted with clay, made these youngsters appear a terrifying gang. Their language was vile, but they were irresistibly attracted by that which met them in the tumble-down old building. They loved to come, and the attendance was soon so large that the next move was to bigger premises still.

This time Mr. Brealey found an old dancing-saloon in Check Street which, though ill-ventilated, was spacious, and connected, by means of a ladder and trap-door, with an upper floor room. In this perilous attic Henrietta conducted the Infant School to which no child over eight years of age was allowed. She stood at the top of the stairs and received her scholars, one by one, from the hands of Mr. Brealey, the Superintendent. Having landed about one hundred of them in safety, Henrietta shut down the trap-door and reigned supreme, oblivious of yells, smells and disturbances. As she herself acknowledged, " It was only by the mercy of God that no accident took place."

Each Sunday evening a Gospel service was held, and this was attended by large numbers of rough, uncouth men and women—a congregation which felt strangely at home in the old dancing-saloon. The preacher was one of themselves, a man they could understand, and the good breeding and courtesy of his helpers solved all problems of class distinction. Thus five years of busy evangelism went by.

Meanwhile there was constant talk in Brethren circles about the claim of heathen lands on the Church. It was taught that the ' rapture of the saints' was to be looked for, yet it was always recognized that 'the Gospel must first be preached as a witness in all lands.'

Practical methods of missionary organization were unknown to them, but earnest individuals were prepared to throw themselves into the breach, and regardless of personal cost set sail to the remote parts of the world. When George Brealey heard of the spiritual destitution in Demerara, he determined to take the Gospel to the negroes of the sugar plantations. His berth was even taken on a sailing vessel, but on the very eve of departure he had the courage to cancel his passage because he saw that his work lay in his native county among the wild Blackdown hills whose population was ignorant, degraded and utterly neglected.

Henrietta was attracted to Burma. Around this mission field her imagination had played since the age of eight when her present from a Christmas tree had been, *The Memoirs of Mrs. Sarah Borden Judson, Missionary in Burma.* Though open to criticism as the choice of a gift for a child, the volume had brought peculiar pleasure to its owner, and the little girl patiently mastered its difficult words and read it from cover to cover, receiving from it a thrill of romance and adventure which, in accordance with family parlance, she spoke of as ' the vision of a poured-out life.' She prayed daily for Burma, and felt that she was doing something definite for that far-off land when she memorised a poem called : " Three Men from Arracan." " All through girlhood the dream of going to Burma as a missionary was with me," she said.

One day, in the spring of 1866, Mr. Soltau came home and immediately called for his daughter.

" Ettie," he said, " I want you and Agnes to go at once to Colonel Smith's house. You will find there a wonderful man. His name is Hudson Taylor ; he is a missionary who has penetrated into the interior of China."

The girls, highly excited, ran off to tie on their bonnets, but before they left the house, he called them back to his room.

"This is a very important event for Exeter," he said. "We must have a good public meeting so that as many people as possible may have the opportunity of hearing what Hudson Taylor has to tell us. I will see about hiring the Athenæum for to-morrow night, and you must be ready to distribute notices and beat up a good attendance."

The two girls were thrilled, for they seldom saw their father so roused by anyone's visit. Knowing nothing of Hudson Taylor's insignificant physique, they pictured him tall, strong and vigorous—in fact, a man whose physical appearance was in proportion to his intrepid spirit. To their surprise, sitting by Colonel Smith's fireside, was a small, quiet and unassuming man, who showed no outward sign of being the great pioneer their father's words had led them to expect. His gentle manner put the two girls completely at their ease, and they were soon deep in talk about the need of the Chinese people.

On the evening of the meeting the hall was packed to overflowing. Dr. Hudson Taylor's text was taken from Proverbs xxiv. 11 : "If thou forbear to deliver them that are drawn unto death and those that are ready to be slain : if thou sayest, Behold, we knew it not, shall not he that pondereth the heart consider it ?" He spoke with great solemnity, and in order to enable his hearers the better to realize the magnitude of the task which lay before the Church in evangelizing so vast a country as China, he used one of his favourite illustrations. "During the brief hour of this meeting," he declared, "more than one thousand of its people have been swept into Christless graves."

The whole audience was impressed, but Henrietta and Agnes Soltau were so profoundly stirred that there was no sleep for them that night. Agnes was to be married the following month, and the result of their long vigil was the decision that the duty of offering for missionary work in China devolved upon Henrietta. Two days later a meeting was arranged in the old dancing hall, where an audience drawn from the slums of Exeter listened to Hudson Taylor speak from Psalm 115, and graphically depict the degradation of the idol worshipper. It was at the close of this meeting that Henrietta offered herself for foreign service, and although her parents thought her too fragile for such a life they would place no obstacle in her path.

The matter was still under consideration when she had a strange experience. She was taken suddenly ill and became unconscious, while her family gathered around believing her to be dying. As she lay, a spiritual vision was given her which she described as follows : " I entered a valley which was very dark and bordered by steep hills on each side. The words which came to my lips were, ' Yea, though I walk through the Valley of the Shadow of Death, I will fear no evil : for Thou art with me.' Though I felt the presence of my Lord I could not see His face. Suddenly I became aware of a bright light, and I saw again the Heavenly City as I had seen it in a dream in childhood. With joy I ran to the gate, but the Lord restrained me and said : ' Not yet, my child, I still have work for you to do. You have yet to learn how to be expert in spiritual warfare.' As these words ' expert in warfare' sounded in my ears, I opened my eyes to see my mother and sister weeping by my side, but I was able instantly to assure them that I should live and not die. During the weakness of the following days I was constantly enquiring of God what that ' warfare' might be to which He had appointed me."

Such an experience of physical weakness caused her offer for work in China to be temporarily in abeyance, and she resumed her former life and activities. To quote her own words : " For many months afterwards I was constantly sent for to visit the sick and those who were near to death, and I had the joy of leading to Christ all those who did not previously know Him."

V

IN 1868 Mr. Soltau's health began definitely to fail and the doctor pronounced his illness to be creeping paralysis. There was no cure, but country life would be beneficial, therefore a house was taken in Newport near Barnstaple, to which he was moved. Blind and partially paralyzed, he yet earned from the villagers the title of 'the happy old gentleman'.

Newport was spiritually dark. The cottagers were visited only by the Rector's sister, an elderly lady, who was much annoyed when she found the new arrivals trespassing in her parish. Fifty years previously good work had been done there by Major Gordon and his family, but he was now over ninety years of age, and others who had been associated with him were too old or too infirm to carry on the Gospel proclamation. They, however, formed a prayer circle, and were in constant intercession for the spiritual needs of the village. Each member of this group recognized in the coming of Mr. Soltau and his family, the answer to years of prayer.

The house they took was large and very old-fashioned. It held a room with a separate back entrance through an old greenhouse, and this was set apart as a mission room. There was a dedication service when the first meeting was held in November, 1870. It was a great gathering addressed by the evangelist Conner. Ettie and her sisters made the meeting known and villagers poured in until every chair in the house was requisitioned to seat them. Conversions began that same day. One poor woman, who shared a small room in a tiny cottage with a drunkard, came to Christ that night, and a little girl eight years old with tears streaming down her cheeks, was heard to say to her mother: " Oh mother, do let us go to God."

A Women's Bible Class was started and grew rapidly until it reached a membership of one hundred and seventy. It was Henrietta's special work. She was now twenty-seven years of age and, for her, life had but one purpose and ruling passion—to win men and women to Christ. She laboured tirelessly to this end, using every device and sparing no effort to tell the Gospel to all with whom she came in contact.

Again and again she witnessed the miracle of a dead soul receiving life, in response to her exhortation. Strengthened by a background of fervent prayer, cases of increasing difficulty were attacked as experience showed her that with God nothing is impossible. Ettie and her sisters were tireless in following up the contacts made in the Meeting Room, and very soon they had access to most of the cottages and farms. There were a few women, however, who would not receive them. One of these steadily refused for two whole years to come to any meeting and at the end of that time said plainly:

" I've told you I won't come, and I won't. Don't come here bothering me any more. I don't want to see your face again."

To which Ettie answered most patiently: " For two years I have come to your door and invited you to my house. Do come just once, to please me."

" If I did," said the woman, " you would only be asking me to come again."

" No," answered Henrietta, " if you come once I promise never to bother you again."

The bargain was struck, the woman would come once and Henrietta would leave her alone.

That evening the woman, true to her side of the compact, arrived, but she stepped into an atmosphere so charged with prayer and faith, that, at the close, she whispered to Henrietta, " Come and see me to-morrow." The next morning it was a changed woman who opened the door and drew the visitor in, with the words: " I'm saved, but I don't know how."

Such incidents so braced her faith that gradually the line of demarcation between the natural and what would be termed miraculous ceased to exist.

She learned in simple confidence to look for events which would have staggered those whom she regarded as teachers.

Without knowing it, she was receiving a special training for a special work. Her motives were so pure and spirit so remarkably translucent, her personality so charming and refined, that opposition was overcome by her mere presence. Her confidence in the origin of the message she was bound to deliver, gave her a boldness which disarmed the critic and broke down the defences of opposition. Instances were multiplied in which ingenuity was carried to its extreme lengths in seeking an entrance to hostile houses when she was convinced that some-one there was needing her message. To quote but one :

In the village there lived a bed-ridden man. All efforts to gain access to him completely failed, owing to the determination of his wife that no member of this Soltau family, which was turning the place upside down, should be admitted. From Henrietta's side it was a simple matter to make friends with children who had access to the house, but every effort to use them as heralds of peace was quickly detected and frustrated by the sharp-witted woman.

The milkman, however, had recently been con-verted, and he was a willing party to Henrietta's schemes. A council of war was held, and the

milkman was commissioned to convey some carefully selected tracts and books which might prove
acceptable in an isolated sickroom. Complete
failure attended this effort. The milk was received,
but the tracts flung out and the door slammed.
Henrietta, the milkman and the children were all
uncompromisingly rebuffed and told to mind their
own business. The triumphant woman lifted the
drawbridge of her castle and congratulated herself
on sufficient strength of mind to keep all these
interferers and religious people at bay, but she little
knew that the forces against which she flung herself
were mighty to the casting down of strongholds.

Nothing daunted, Henrietta committed her cause
to God and with ingenuity, illuminated by insight,
set to work to attack the citadel once more. One
summer morning she walked in the old-world
garden where the luxuriant vegetation and beautiful
flowers delighted the eye, while the singing of the
birds and the beautiful sunshine flooded her heart
with joy and exhilaration. To her, everything spoke
of God and communion with Him was the natural
expression of her joy.

Meanwhile her tenacious will was subconsciously
forming plans for reaching that bed-ridden man
who was denied all that she so keenly enjoyed. Why
should he not share the Father's bounty even if he
refused the Father's love? A basket was prepared,
filled with the very best fruit of the garden and

decorated with some of its choicest flowers. With a flash of inspiration she cut slips of paper on which she wrote verses from the Bible, and round the stem of each blossom, as though to protect the fruit from injury, she carefully wound the messages. There lay before her a fragrant spray of scarlet geranium and a pure white rose. These two she bound together with a slip on which was written : "Though your sins be as scarlet, they shall be as white as snow."

A child was easily found to carry the anonymous gift to the door and the woman, quite off her guard, accepted for the invalid luxuries which she herself was unable to provide for him. With delight the sick man lifted the fruit from the basket, inhaled the perfume of the flowers, welcoming the diversion by which the weary monotony of the day was unexpectedly broken. As he removed the paper from the stem of each flower, his eye caught the written words : "Though your sins be as scarlet, they shall be as white as snow." With tremendous power a sense of the immanence of God assailed his soul. His sins were as scarlet, was it true that they might yet be as white as snow ? He called to his wife, asking who had left the flowers ? The sender must be found and brought to his bedside.

"Little Nellie brought them round," was the answer, but, seeing the texts lying on the quilt, she guessed that Henrietta Soltau was behind it. Her fury knew no bounds, especially as her husband demanded that she bring the young lady to his bedside.

When Ettie entered his room she saw that pure white rose and the scarlet geranium lying side by side; using them as a text, she led the anxious man to his Saviour. An hour later, when she left the room, all was changed for him and his liberated being thrilled in response to the touch of new life. Even the wife's resentful attitude was gradually changed as she saw the transformation in her husband, the more so as his physical condition rapidly improved and there was hope of better days. Ettie became a welcome visitor to the house and eventually had the joy of leading the wife also to the Saviour's feet.

There was joy in the presence of the angels of God over sinners repenting, but there was contention and resentment among the ' righteous ' in Newport on account of the liberties taken by the Soltau family in visiting the sick and dying, among the cottagers. This, they considered, should only be done by the clergy or by those whom they appointed.

The Rector's sister was so angry that she went direct to Mrs. Soltau and asked her to forbid her young people from interfering in the parish. Mrs. Soltau was so courteous and gracious in her reception, and explained her point of view with such earnest conviction, that the Rector's sister was almost conciliated. She even left the house with a bundle of Mr. Soltau's booklets in her hand. These writings were used to open her eyes to spiritual values. She became a friend and ceased to view the work of the Soltau family as an encroachment on parochial rights.

VI

IN the natural course of events the young members of the family began to scatter.

Before they left Exeter for Newport, Agnes had married Richard Hill. Now George secured a post in London in the Civil Service, and not long afterwards Henry followed him there, having found an opening in an accountant's office.

Lucy, eldest of the family, felt within herself the capacity for filling a much wider sphere than she found at Newport. The restrictions of Brethrenism lay irksomely on her, for although they allowed her to visit, to preach to individuals both men and women, and to teach the Bible to a large class of boys, yet directly preaching was addressed to an audience, or teaching was directed to a congregation, she was under a ban which silenced her.

From earliest years their friend Fanny Fitzgerald was an ideal to the Soltau girls. She was a constant visitor in their home, and on the occasion of her marriage to Dr. Grattan Guinness it was Mr. Soltau who, as closest friend, gave her away.

Lucy, Henrietta and Agnes had been their father's trusted lieutenants in open-air evangelism ever since the time when little Ettie clung to her father's leg through a shower of cabbage stalks and rotten eggs in the slums of Plymouth. No insults ever deterred these plucky girls from supporting the Brethren in open-air meetings, both in town and village. Yet though they might organize the choir they must never sing a solo, and though they might act as target for the cabbage-stalks, might not tell the crowd why they placed themselves in such an uncomfortable position.

At this time letters reached Newport from Fanny Grattan Guinness, telling that she had 'broken *her* bonds asunder' and was conducting open-air services in the slums of Bath, assisted by a woman friend. Their testimony had been 'signally owned and blessed by God,' and there were many conversions to report. Mr. Soltau's daughters were thrilled by her courage and though, as dutiful girls, they bowed to their father's commands, his judgment was no longer unquestioned. Doubts as to the legitimacy of the restrictions placed on them, stirred the depths of their souls. Some such questionings must also have germinated in the honest mind of Mr. Soltau, for, after this, when speakers were not forthcoming to conduct evangelistic meetings he would suggest that one of the girls should give the address.

"Father," Henrietta once asked, "why do you ask me to address the Meeting, when you always taught us that a woman must not speak in public?"

"This is different—the Gospel," was his abrupt answer.

Yet, at first, neither of the girls ventured to break the habit of years and they only spoke under their father's immediate direction. Not until 1882 did Henrietta, to use her own words, " launch out into a fuller life, publicly and freely preaching Christ."

George and Henry came home for holidays and brought reports of evangelism in London slums which set Newport on fire. There the work was both difficult and dangerous, the children of the ragged schools with which they were connected being drawn from the worst alleys in Clerkenwell, known as Jack Ketch's Warren, a resort of thieves avoided by the police.

The girls longed to have a share and decided that one way in which they might help would be to pick flowers and make them into small bunches, each tied up with a hand-printed text. The recently converted village carpenter made suitable boxes for conveying them to London, where the brothers used them to effect an entrance to sordid homes.

Lucy was a highly gifted girl and easily leader in the family circle. Picking flowers and printing texts seemed childish work to a woman in whose bones the fire burnt. She was weary with forbearing and her letters, written at this time, show her craving "to be released from the littleness of things." Stirring within her was the capacity to handle big issues, and the constant restrictions placed on her, both in social and religious life, thwarted and irritated her.

On March 30th, 1873, Lucy was taken ill with
pneumonia following on rheumatic fever and
disease of the heart. On April 7th all hope of her
recovery was abandoned and her brothers were
summoned from London by telegram. Finding
that they had been called home, she knew that she
was expected to die.

" I cannot believe that I am to be taken now,"
she said, " it is such a wonderful hour in which to
live and work for Christ. If two or three of us
agree to pray for my recovery, I shall surely be
healed."

Her friends surrounded her with tender love
but with a passivity which shut the very winds of
God from her soul.

" If you were ill," she said to one of them,
" would you not send for the elders of the church
and expect recovery ? "

" No, dear," was the answer, " I have lived too
long in this wilderness to desire life."

Lucy's whole soul revolted at an attitude which
could speak so gloomily of the precious heritage
of life. As the disease made rapid progress she
tried to rouse her friends to action and the atmosphere of resignation seemed to smother her. The
approach of death brought her no fear, only
distress lest her labour for Christ be curtailed.

Her mother saw she was sinking and thought
that Robert Chapman might help to illumine for

her some of the mysteries which troubled her. He came, sat by her bedside and talked with her.

"Lucy," he said, "we do not know the nature of service in heaven, but God calls His people each at the moment He needs them, so that I am never surprised at Christians of any age departing."

Lucy was more settled in her mind after this visit, but the acute stage of the heart disease was rapidly developing and her sufferings intensified. For several hours of the following day her six brothers and sisters sat round her bedside praying with her and repeating words of comfort from the Scriptures. Thus the last day of her life on earth passed, and towards evening she watched the setting sun and said : "When you see it rise again think of me in the presence of the Lord Jesus, beholding His face." On Good Friday morning, at one o'clock, she breathed her last with the words : "The Lord is calling me . . . now." When the sun streamed in at the window her family remembered her words and were comforted.

On the day of the funeral more than one thousand of those who loved her assembled at the graveside. For over an hour there was preaching.

Every member of her Lads' Class came to Christ and many of them became earnest workers for the Lord, subsequently devoting their lives to the preaching of the Gospel. Before her death she arranged for the distribution of her personal possessions and left this Will : " My sermon books to George and Henry, my music books to Charlotte, my little desk for Agnes, my dolls' tea set for Mary. There are not many clothes but let them go to poor old Miss Coombes. I should like each boy in my class to have a Bible but I cannot remember how much money there is—perhaps not enough."

In accordance with the strangely intimate expression of the period, a small book was compiled by her brothers and sisters in which they wrote down the detailed record of Lucy's last week on earth and every word of their conversations.

The shock of her death told so severely on her father that he never left his room again, and, two years later, he also died.   Meanwhile, at much sacrifice, Henry threw up his appointment in London in order to be at home. The work of village evangelism, however, derived fresh vigour from his presence, and each week he spoke in the Mission Hall and as opportunity occurred conducted farmhouse services.

Life resumed its even tenor until 1875 which proved to be, for the Soltau family, a year of momentous happenings. Events followed thick and fast which broke up the peaceful home, scattering its inmates far and wide. Their message to Newport was delivered, their diverging paths of service determined, and streams of life were now to flow through them to the uttermost parts of the earth.

THE WINGS OF THE MORNING

I

AFTER Lucy's death Henry was unable to take up work in London again. Home claims remained insistent, and his mother was dependent on him for advice in daily concerns, as well as for conducting the evangelistic work which, to the Soltau family, was the foremost business of life.

Two busy years went by, filled with every kind of religious activity. In 1875 he took scarlet fever, and when he had recovered, went to Hastings for convalescence. In Hastings he had a very remarkable experience. It was here that the claim of God for absolute obedience to the Divine will was laid on him to an extent he had not realized before. Henry's answer was " Yea, Lord," but through a memorable night, the pressure on his spirit kept him facing the possible implications of entire surrender. Daybreak found him broken but triumphant. The early post solved for him the riddle of God's peculiar dealings, for, on the breakfast table, was a letter from Dr. Hudson Taylor.

For some time the matter of entrance to the western province of Yünnan, had been one of Hudson Taylor's deepest concerns. It seemed impossible to reach that distant border from the China side, therefore it was decided to accept the offer of John Stevenson, a member of the China Inland Mission, to attempt an entrance by an untried road through Burma. Hudson Taylor with five other men prayed for wisdom in the conduct of this great pioneering journey, and specially asked that God would let them know who was the companion to be chosen to share the danger with John Stevenson.

The six men rose from their knees each one individually convinced that Henry Soltau was God's choice. After mature consideration Hudson Taylor wrote and laid the whole case before him. The letter was travelling to Hastings during the night when Henry Soltau said " Yea, Lord " to God's mysterious demands. He went straight back to Newport and told his mother all about it.

" What have you to say, Mother ? " he asked. " My own answer has gone, telling Dr. Taylor that God had commissioned me before ever his letter was in my hands."

" My child," was her answer, " your father and I did solemnly declare unto God that we would never hinder any child of ours in obeying His commands."

Thus the matter was clinched.

During the busy days of outfitting, packing and farewells, Henry was publicly commended to God by D. L. Moody at the Agricultural Hall where the Evangelistic Meetings were held. One month to the day, from his Hastings experience Henry Soltau sailed from Glasgow for the Far East.

His father was never even aware that he had gone, and only a few weeks later Mrs. Soltau and her children were standing round the grave in which his earthly remains were laid. Shortly afterwards the old house was sold, and Mrs. Soltau removed her furniture to Tottenham, where she made her home.

Henrietta was thirty-two years old, and she was free. What should her life-work be? Her own hope was that she might be strong enough for China, but when, on a visit to Dr. and Mrs. Hudson Taylor in London, she was prostrated by one of the worst attacks of headache she had had, the doctor shook his head, and the long-cherished plan was finally vetoed.

Before the close of the visit, however, there was light for her on the next step of her path. It was a day of rapid advance in missionary societies. Many suitable men and women were offering themselves, evidently called to the work of world-wide evangelism, but there was immediate need for organization within the societies to facilitate the forward trend of events.

The immediate question was how to supply a home-life for missionaries' children while their parents were abroad. Dr. Hudson Taylor, with characteristic foresight, would not wait until difficulties had arisen before providing against such a need. Henrietta Soltau seemed pre-ordained to the execution of his plan. She was a woman whose breeding and personal character could not fail to commend her to all with whom she came in contact. He saw in her the ideal head of a house which would be 'home' to the young children of the missionaries. Leaving them in her care, the parents' hearts would be completely at rest, and their minds, relieved of all anxiety, would be set free for the work abroad.

The financial basis of the proposed scheme was thoroughly discussed, and Henrietta Soltau, for the first time, saw Hudson Taylor put into action the principles of dependence on God which governed his rules of conduct.

A small sum of money was available for the enterprise. It was not much over a hundred pounds, and little enough for all there was to do. Hudson Taylor, however, was certain that God had directed the opening of the home, and he launched forth in confidence that all needful supplies would be forthcoming. Henrietta, as yet, knew but little of such ventures of faith, but was equally certain of being in the line of God's will when she accepted the position of head. She was, however, strongly discouraged from doing so by various friends, among whom were those whose advice she valued.

A house was taken in the quiet, healthy surroundings of Tottenham. It was called Copnor House, and a great friend offered to join her, bringing furniture and two servants. This solved one of the initial problems. The household was completed by eight children, both boys and girls.

Seeing that the parents were not receiving a stated salary they were unable to promise any definite sum towards the support of their children, though it was understood that they would honourably contribute as they were able.

Henrietta Soltau was now to become one of those who receive daily bread direct from the Father's Hand. Many were the lessons previously mastered in the school of faith, but she had never shared in this particular covenant. The life of the community was sustained by agencies which worked in obedience to a spiritual plan known only to those who were called to form part of it. One restriction which she felt compelled to place on herself was that her needs be told to no human friend. Even her mother, desirous as she was to share the life of her daughter, might not know the secrets of this particular experience. Henrietta Soltau herself wrote of this period: " This was my training school. I was ignorant and unfit for such a work, but I saw how Dr. Hudson Taylor trusted in God and how God sustained him, so I was encouraged to do the same."

To no one has this lesson proved easy, and though at first all went well, the hundred pounds gradually dwindled without showing any sign of replenishment. However, her friend was there, the servants and their wages were assured, and Henrietta went forward in bright confidence. The testing began when the friend herself developed small-pox, after nursing a relative through that illness. The health officer was summoned, and the sick woman taken off to the nearest isolation hospital, where in due course she recovered, though the officer who removed her from the house took the disease and died, it being of a peculiarly virulent form.

When all seemed serene once more, a relative died leaving a family of orphan children dependent on her, so that, at short notice, she was compelled to leave Copnor House, taking the servants and furniture with her. Further inroads had to be made into the diminished capital in order to buy chairs, tables and beds for the empty rooms, and still no supplies came in. At last only five pounds remained in hand, and Henrietta was faced with a claim for six pounds, eighteen shillings and two-pence for rates.

Under covenant to share this burden with no human being, she entered upon the severest test of her life of faith. She could not but question whether the whole undertaking had been a mistake.

Her best friends had not been in sympathy with the establishment of the home, and had warned her against being too strongly influenced by the 'fanaticism' of such men as Hudson Taylor and George Müller. They had also told her that she must not count on them should the scheme prove a failure. Giant Despair brought all these things vividly to her mind during her imprisonment in Doubting Castle. It seemed at this hour that her friends' warnings were fully justified. The five pounds were gradually spent on necessary food for the family, and but few days remained before the rate-collector was to call for the six pounds, eighteen shillings and twopence, which she seemed totally unable to supply.

On Friday afternoon she presided at the children's tea, they, perfectly satisfied with the simple fare, prattling happily to her and to each other, she sitting behind the urn and making a meal of dry bread. A ring at the door-bell announced the arrival of a caller. It was an elderly lady whom she met each Sunday at the Brook Street Brethren Meeting. She was not an attractive person, and her visit at this time was the less welcome in that she immediately set to work to enquire "how the faith programme is working out."

"Is there sufficient to meet obligations? If so, why did you look so worn at the Sunday morning Assembly of Saints?" she asked; then, looking inquisitively around, " I should like to know how much money there is in the house at this very moment."

The whole attitude was that of an experienced mother in Israel admonishing a wayward girl who set herself up to interpret the leadings of God in a manner unbecoming to youth and to feminine disability. Such a cross-examination was intensely painful at this moment of strain, and Henrietta's one desire was to bring the interview to a speedy close. She was determined not to gratify her visitor's curiosity, so, by way of diversion, tried to induce her to come and join the children, but this strategy was ruthlessly foiled.

" I don't want to see the children," she snapped. " I have come for a good talk with you."

Then, seeing Henrietta's distress, and the difficulty with which she controlled her voice, she suddenly changed her tone.

" There, there, my dear, don't cry, I was only teasing you. I really came to tell you that two weeks ago a small sum of money came to me unexpectedly, and I was sure that I ought to donate it to your home. I put off doing so from day to day, but here it is at last."

With this she laid on the table the sum of six pounds, eighteen shillings and two pence. At the sight of that exact sum, with the two coppers lying on top, Henrietta's self-control broke down, and she wept. The amount due for rates was supplied to within a penny. This sign was as certain a confirmation of God's approval on her manner of life as was the fleece to Gideon, or the budding of Aaron's rod to Moses.

Henrietta Soltau, in her later experiences, knew many dark days and stood many severe tests, but there was that in the particular provision of the sum for which she had cried so insistently to God, which was a message from Jehovah to her, His helpless child, assuring her that nothing which was big to her could be small to Him. Here was the ratification of God's side of the covenant, without which her test would have been beyond human strength. It was the living declaration of the familiar words : " Fear not, for I am with thee."

The bonds of Giant Despair were broken, the walls of Doubting Castle shook to their foundation, and Henrietta stepped out free.

For three years Miss Soltau continued at Copnor House, taking an ever increasing share in the general work necessitated by the rapid growth of the China Inland Mission. Every moment that could be spared was devoted to secretarial work or accounts, but the most enduring feature of all that was inaugurated at that period has been the weekly Prayer Meeting, which continues vigorous to this day. Every Saturday afternoon Henrietta Soltau and her friend laid aside all other work in order

to pray for China. Sixty years have passed and
the Prayer Meeting for China continues. Until
physical weakness made attendance impossible,
Miss Soltau was never missing from her seat in
that weekly gathering.

II

THE number of children grew to twelve. Some were from China, others from Penang and Demerara, and their ages ranged from three to nine years. One of them, nearly sixty years later, writes : " We were most of us ill, and very naughty, owing to the climate and surroundings in which we had been born. Miss Soltau's hands were very full day and night for, with the help of a governess and later a nurse, she did everything for us."

One of the children suffered from a skin disease contracted in the tropics which soon infected the whole group, and it became necessary for Miss Soltau and the children to isolate themselves rigidly. The doctors gave but little hope of permanent cure and the verdict of one was, " You might as well try to cure the children of leprosy." All the then known remedies were perseveringly applied and many hours each day were spent on treatments which, though beneficial to the children, were often wearying to the patience of those who looked after them.

The atmosphere of prayer which Miss Soltau breathed, commended itself to her small charges and they recognized every event of life as directly and intimately arranged for them by the Father in Heaven Whose will was always good and therefore must be acceptable. Subtler problems, which so often confuse the adult mind, had not, in these early days, invaded their mental vision and Miss Soltau's own outlook was no less childlike and un-questioning than that of the little sufferer who, at the age of six, was saying: "I am sure that God will not let me be ill like this all my life."

Miss Soltau's devotion during these difficult years was unsurpassed. Never for a moment could those children suspect that their presence was anything but a joy to her, nor could they imagine what the treatment of this revolting disease was costing her. Her own hand became poisoned by the infection and she had to carry on her duties with her fingers strapped to a metal plate.

One writes : " Miss Soltau always had wonderful ideas for making Sunday a different day from all others and yet a very happy day for even the little ones ; but it cost her a great deal of time and thought. Our puzzles and games were all to do with Scripture, and different clothes and food marked it out. One four-year-old from Spain, a few years later, described it as 'Egg-day, cake-day, tea-day.'"

Another, writing after many years of silence, said : "My memory of everything before my

return to China in 1886 is very faint now . . .
but you stand out most clearly. I can just remember Wellington Square and Fairy Glen. The hap-
piest memories of my childhood are always of
picking flowers in the country. . . . When my
dear old Daddy died, I went through his correspondence and found a number of your letters.
. . . I did not realize until I read them, how much
love you had given to my childhood. Children are
often ungrateful through ignorance. . . ."

Owing to the delicacy of the children it was
thought wise to take them to live at the seaside,
and the whole family was moved to Dovercourt
where they spent eighteen months before finally
settling down at Hastings. Thanks to long hours
of play on the beach and sea-bathing, the children's
physical condition rapidly improved. One by one
they were healed of the troublesome skin disease
until even the child who had introduced it to the
house, and whose case the doctor declared to be
quite hopeless, was well. It was a glorious day for
the family when the doctor pronounced her free
of infection and the children, after four years'
quarantine, could once more mix freely with
others.

At Dovercourt the beach services were a great
delight to the children. One day the preacher
asked if any child present could repeat the 119th
Psalm. He doubtless felt confident that no one

would respond, but, to his surprise, a long row of children, sitting well to the front, instantly held up their hands. He thought they had misunderstood the question and referred to the lady who brought them. She told him it was quite true that they could recite that long Psalm, beside many others. Next day he called at the house and they all stood in a row and repeated it to him. The children not only memorized Scripture, but were taught to apply it in ways that were sometimes delightful. One of them writes : " When we helped the cook to prepare fruit for jam-making, we were always allowed to pick out a share for ourselves, because the Bible says, ' Thou shalt not muzzle the mouth of the ox that treadeth out the corn,' and ' The workman is worthy of his meat.' "

Miss Soltau's birthday was always celebrated by a children's party at which they were allowed to use the beautiful tea-set which had been given her when she was seven years old by her grandfather's faithful servant, William Challice. While at Dovercourt the lease of the house at Tottenham expired, and Miss Soltau's mother suggested that no more healthy place could be found for the children than Hastings, where she was herself living.

The proposal commended itself to Henrietta and she arranged to go down and see a vacant house which seemed suitable. In connection with this an incident occurred, small in itself, but of a kind constantly afforded her in order to strengthen her faith along the particular line of training to which she was being subjected. On the day fixed for the expedition there was only money enough in the house for the single fare and sixpence over. However, many experiences had taught her that necessary means were often not supplied until the moment at which they were required.

She bought her ticket, and started for Hastings with sixpence in her pocket. The house was suitable, so she made application for it, and when her business was finished, prepared for the return journey. As she left her mother's house Mrs. Soltau said: " Ettie, I am going to pay your fare to London. Now mind, this is an extra for yourself, not to be spent on those children."

With a silent acknowledgment of the Father's care she took the amount and with it bought her ticket. The sixpence was still at the bottom of her purse and though she knew that some fresh provision must be made to get her from London to Dovercourt, she proceeded on her journey with a mind sufficiently at leisure to be occupied with plans for the projected move to Hastings, untroubled by financial strain. At Victoria station she met her sister Agnes and they spent some time talking over family matters. In the course of conversation Agnes said:

" I have ten pounds in my pocket for you which was given to me yesterday."

So it was that during those expensive days many extra gifts came, enabling her to meet all liabilities and also the expenses of moving into the new house which she had seen in Wellington Square.

III

THE following nine years cover the rest of the time during which Miss Soltau took charge of missionaries' children. They were spent in Hastings. In all, thirty-two children passed through her hands, including many whose parents were not associated with the China Inland Mission.

Miss Soltau herself records that at this time she had ceased to bear any anxiety regarding money matters. "Once only during my stay in Hastings were my funds reduced to less than a shilling." Early or late, provision was always made in time to meet family needs. The children attended a school which was conveniently close at hand, and here the very little ones helped to swell the ranks of the Kindergarten.

One writes: "Much of her time was spent in correspondence with missionaries in all parts of the world and their letters were read aloud to us. Not only did we learn to know the missionaries through their letters, but many stayed in our home as visitors; among them, Mrs. Huntley, from Demerara; Mr. Alfred Laker and his daughter from the Cameroons; Dr. and Mrs. Henry Soltau from Burma; Mr. and Mrs. Baldwin from N. Africa (six of whose children were left under

Miss Soltau's care). There was also Mr. Craven from the Congo, with six-year-old Topsy, whom he and his wife had adopted, and with whom we loved to play. One day at dinner she made a remark, and when we asked what she had said Mr. Craven only laughed. We would not be satisfied until he interpreted : ' All these children put their noses in their glasses when they drink.' The fact was that someone had teased her about her own little flattened nose which was supposed to stay outside the tumbler while she drank."

Miss Soltau possessed to an unsuspected degree the gift of the novelist. As a girl one of her secret indulgences had been to lie awake at night weaving romantic plots and curiously enough, in later life, during long periods of agonising headache, she found relief in giving rein to her talent for fiction. Among children she let herself go and many a wet Saturday afternoon, surrounded by a circle of small, eager listeners, she would tell stories for hours, making the time pass with almost equal enjoyment both to the teller and to the hearers. Such a gift would not have been smiled on by the Brethren Assembly, even though she only indulged it among children. The time came, however, when, seeking for deeper religious experience than she had yet known, the shadow of her early training fell across the resilience of her spirit, and from that hour she allowed herself no further indulgence of this kind.

Thereafter the children's eager demand for 'more stories,' was met only with Bible and missionary incidents though they included, of course, the gems of fiction which have been sanctified as coming from the lips of Jesus Himself. The art of the teller was still there, however, and many Scriptural incidents which would have seemed remote from other lips, became living as she told them. What she gained spiritually is sacred to herself and to God.

The following incident will serve to illustrate with what simplicity and understanding the children shared the atmosphere of faith which pervaded the house and how, to the little ones, it was part of the interest of life to pray for things and watch for the answer to come. There was one member of the household, however, who considered this 'faith business' a most unsatisfactory basis for housekeeping, though she could but say that food had never been short or her wages overdue. It was Lydia, the servant maid, who was passionately devoted to her mistress in a troublesome and hysterical fashion. She would have liked to surround Miss Soltau with luxuries, attentions and comforts which evidently formed no part of the Divine programme. On one occasion when she was taking supper to the bedside of a sick child,

the little patient began prattling to her about
Christmas and the beautiful puddings they would
have. Lydia flatly answered :

" There ain't going to be no pudding. Miss
Soltau's too poor to buy currants and raisins."

The child, though slightly staggered, rose to the
occasion and caught Lydia on her unguarded
flank.

" Lydia," she said, " let's have a secret. When
you bring up my tray in the evening we will pray
for currants, and see if they come. Don't let's tell
anyone."

Lydia entered into the compact with great delight,
for it exactly suited her to be promoted to the
position of intercessor for family needs. If currants
came (and experience had taught her that these
things did happen), with what pride she would
view her own share in the transaction ! The two
conspirators prayed secretly and vigorously, but
nothing happened and Christmas was close at hand
before any answer came.

One evening Miss Soltau returned at midnight
from taking her share in nursing her sick mother,
to find the excited Lydia panting on the doorstep.

" Please, ma'am, there's a parcel come, and I
think it's the currants. The man just put it down
and went away."

Miss Soltau, accustomed to the girl's excitable
ways, suppressed her.

"I am expecting parcels for China," she said, "leave them in the hall and go to bed. You should have been there long ago."

She then went to her study to write a few letters, but, looking up, found Lydia at her side once more, this time sobbing.

"Oh, Miss, please, do open the parcel. I can't sleep till I know if it's the currants."

Miss Soltau, knowing nothing of the prayer compact, was inclined to treat the whole matter with a firm hand, but Lydia, between her sobs, blurted out the whole story, and, together, they opened the parcel to find twenty pounds weight of currants. Now they were both excited and arranged that nothing should be said to the children until they were gathered for prayers. Then the bale would be produced.

The little sick girl, wrapped in her dressing-gown, was carried downstairs, and a yell of joy greeted the sight of the mountain of dried fruit. Lydia's face shone with consequential pride at her share in this supply of family needs. With a trace of awe at the stupendous miracle, her little partner in prayer clapped her hands and said :

"You see, Lydia, I *knew* God would send it."

When the uproar was over and the thanksgivings had been rendered, Miss Soltau reminded them that a pudding cannot be made of currants alone, and together, in prayer, they enumerated before their

Heavenly Father the ingredients still required, flour, sugar, spice, suet, raisins, etc. The days before Christmas were few, but every day the children's first question on rushing in from school was :

" Has the pudding come yet ? "

Just before Christmas it did come and it was on this wise : The family was assembled at evening prayers and Miss Soltau was in the midst of reading a Psalm when a knock came to the door. Charlie boldly interrupted the reading, saying :

" Perhaps it's the pudding."

Lydia went to open the door, and returned dragging a large hamper, at the sight of which Charlie yelled :

" Put away the Bibles, it's the pudding."

With shouts of delight the basket was opened and found to contain all that was needed for Christmas puddings with oranges and cakes for the whole party. Lydia professed herself a thorough convert to the power of prayer and from this time onward she never again questioned the principles on which the house was run. There was no clue to the sender, for the man had handed the hamper in saying : " There is no name and no answer."

There were instances when no clue was forthcoming as to the source of supply. In this case, however, it was otherwise. Five months later Miss Soltau was fighting her way, after dark, against a south-west gale, to reach the pillar-box.

Here she met a lady bent on the same errand as herself, who seemed too frail to resist the elements. Miss Soltau, though she knew her by sight as a resident of Wellington Square, did not know her name, but offered to see her home. The lady gratefully accepted her help and, in the course of conversation, enquired :

" Are you not the lady who lives with all the little children ? "

" I am," said Miss Soltau. " Their parents are missionaries."

The lady seemed much interested and said : " I should take this opportunity of apologising to you for sending round, without a word of explanation, a bale of currants. My husband has relatives in Spain who sent him a large consignment of dried fruits last Christmas, far too much for our small household to consume. My husband and I often watch the children running to school and I said : ' That is the kind of household that could dispose of a bale of currants,' so we just sent them round."

" You can scarcely believe what joy they gave to my little family," said Miss Soltau.

The conversation was interrupted by overwhelming gusts of wind, but the lady managed to explain that after sending such a large consignment of currants, she felt a strong desire to supply all that was necessary for the children's Christmas treat and so the second parcel had been dispatched.

" You must forgive me," she said, " for the way in which it was done, but not having the pleasure of your acquaintance, I scarcely knew how to offer a present to the children unless it were sent anonymously. Now I have met you I hope to have the pleasure of calling upon you."

Before they parted Miss Soltau requested that her little charges be allowed to call and thank her in person, so next day all the children, dressed in their best and having each learnt an appropriate text, walked across the Square and were admitted to the room where Mr. Kay, who was an invalid, lay on the sofa. He was deeply interested in Miss Soltau's side of the story and affected at the sight of all these children to whom, at such small cost to himself, he had given such immense pleasure. He enquired concerning the parents of each and heard that afternoon some stories of heroic self-sacrifice.

Once the ice was broken there was no stopping the children's prattle and he soon learnt the story of little Emma and her rheumatic fever, of Lydia's bold unbelief and of the prayer for currants and the wonderful answer. Mr. Kay was a product of the nineteenth century school of thought which saw in science the inevitable denial of Providence. The line of demarcation between a Christian and an unbeliever was, in those days, clearly outlined and men who disbelieved in God were not afraid to style themselves atheists. Mr. Kay, who openly ranged himself on the side of the free-thinkers, saw before him a woman whose face radiated a heavenly light, a group of children who persistently regarded him as a messenger of God and, in the background, he pictured that heroic band of parents prepared to make any sacrifice for the faith which he denied.

The man who said in his heart, " There is no God ", became aware of His presence in such compelling terms that the strongly constructed citadel of unbelief within him crumbled, and, for the first time in his life, he bowed in spirit before the God Whom he had denied.

IV

ON the last day of 1881 Henrietta Soltau sat alone by the fire, reviewing the year so nearly closed. The children were in bed; she was free to think her own thoughts safe from their observant eyes, and was too much preoccupied to light the gas. It was an hour of painful self-examination, yet she was courageous enough to allow herself leisure and solitude to review in detail the dealings of God since she entered upon the covenant of faith.

There had been many testings, shortness of funds and wearing perplexities, but she had learnt, once for all, that God having undertaken to supply the family with daily bread, it could never fail. Yet her innermost feeling was a deep sense of failure and short-coming. To use her own words, she saw herself 'lacking at every point.'

To a woman of her spiritual sincerity a sense of failure could never be made an occasion for silencing the inward voice by increased outward activity. She had sighted higher ground, and the result was an inward questioning as to whether she still maintained the fervour characteristic of those active and satisfying years at Newport.

She recalled the old days, men and women brought to Christ, the large Bible Class, visits to the sick

and dying, and the inspiring hope of being herself
a missionary to the heathen. During recent years her
life had ceased to bear such evidences of God's
blessing. It was circumscribed by the few small
children, their frequent illnesses, the long quaran-
tines after infectious diseases, the details of their
school-life, feeding, clothing, accounts, Lydia's
tantrums. All these things took on a sordid
aspect in that lonely vigil. Her own health was
less good than formerly, she was more frequently
prostrated by headaches. Was this the result of
spiritual loss ? Had she now the necessary vitality
to attempt that which she had once compassed
with ease ? A knock at the door roused her. It
was a friend fetching her for the midnight service.
She made no move to light the gas, glad to hide
her tear-stained face, but she stirred the fire and
asked her friend to sit down.

"I have come to ask your help," her visitor
began, "for I cannot face another year under the
sense of spiritual failure with which this one closes.
I am sure you can help me, because you are so
different yourself."

"How little you know me," answered Miss
Soltau. "I have been sitting here reviewing my
own life, and like you I see failure everywhere."

An hour later they parted. Each had shared her
burden with the other and been encouraged by the
sense of companionship. A resolution was made

that every Monday afternoon, at three o'clock, they would meet for prayer. Others might be invited who, like themselves, hungered for a deeper knowledge of God. This prayer-meeting, which began with an attendance of four, grew from week to week. By June the room was filled with those who were of one heart and one mind.

One of the group read the life of Frances Ridley Havergal, and all eagerly discussed the story of a hungry soul who found satisfaction through a spiritual experience which she called the 'second blessing.' The term itself was anathema to the Brethren, but it exactly represented the experience which they coveted.

This circle of praying people in Hastings was feeling its way to a knowledge of the truth which would transform failure into victory. That person of the Trinity called so conventionally in the Churches " The Holy Ghost, the Comforter," was revealing Himself to them as the Lord and Giver of Life.

Miss Soltau describes the experience of those days in the following words : " I felt under the search-light of the Holy God, and I cried in secret for deliverance from inward sin, but my condition seemed to get worse. My physical strength was failing, the headaches increased, and I spent days and nights in acute suffering. Above all a sense of the pressure of sin and failure was perpetually upon my spirit."

At this time she first heard of 'Bethshan, the Home of Healing,' where the restoring power of the all-conquering Christ was claimed in the treatment of human illness.

Henrietta greatly desired to visit Bethshan, which was located in North London, feeling that she might receive there the help she needed for the healing of her physical weakness, and she determined that, if some provision could be made for the childrens' summer holiday, she herself would go to London and seek help. For the first time since she was in charge of the Home invitations came for children to spend the holidays with friends, and a cousin also asked for the loan of the house during their absence. Everything seemed to be arranged for her, and some of the children had already left when little Edith fell ill with scarlet fever. The remainder of the household was quickly scattered, and Miss Soltau, with the help of the young servant girl, prepared herself once more for a long quarantine.

For seven weeks she had no intercourse with the outer world, no one came to the house, and the prayer-meeting stopped abruptly. The strain of nursing brought on a succession of particularly bad headaches, and in an hour of despondency little Edith startled her by voicing her own unexpressed thought : " Why does not God answer prayer ? "

" God does answer prayer," were the words that came instinctively to her lips.

"Then why does not your head get well?" continued the childish philosopher.

The school of thought to which she belonged compelled Miss Soltau to give a conventional and unconvincing reply:

"Well, dear, God does not always answer immediately, we must await His time."

The child was silenced but not satisfied. She felt that she had been bluffed.

The weary weeks of isolation passed. In due time the children returned and all were busy preparing for the routine of winter. On September 20 Miss Soltau was sitting in her study when Lydia announced a visitor. The lady was a stranger to Miss Soltau, and had merely called to ask for an address. However, when the two women faced one another, there was that in her visitor which was so electrifying in its spiritual predominance as to cause Miss Soltau to break through every social convention and without preliminaries say:

"Can you tell me what Frances Ridley Havergal meant when she spoke of a 'second blessing'?"

"Oh yes," was the reply, and the lady proceeded to speak of the liberating power of the Spirit of God in the life and service of the Christian. She explained that where the Spirit of the Lord is there is liberty, freedom from the bondage of sin, from the tyranny of self, from the oppression of fear and from the mastery of Satan. More deeply conscious of sin than ever in her life before, and longing for liberty, Henrietta was struggling against those invisible but most tenacious of all bonds, the prejudices and impressions of early childhood.

"You are unwilling to see where you have been trained in error," said her visitor. "Beware lest you regard the tradition of man as more important than the commandments of God."

Gradually her eyes were opened, and she saw that she had sheltered behind traditions which had become the cerements of her soul. She was silent before her Lord, and in that silence heard Him say : "Loose her and let her go." She arose a free woman.

Left alone she took little account of the passing of time, and was aroused from a condition of intense spiritual consciousness by the sound of the dinner bell. Feeling it essential to secure a few hours of uninterrupted silence in which to readjust her outlook, she proposed to the children that they take their tea in baskets to the sea-shore. With great delight they accepted this unexpected treat, and in solitude she tried to realize the bearing of this new thing that had happened. An ecstasy of joy invaded her soul, and when she came to herself she craved to share her experience with another, so when Lydia came to her room she said :

"My child, although I have been converted for years I never knew such joy as I have experienced to-day."

Lydia, round-eyed with amazement, could only gasp : " My, ain't yer well, Miss ? "

The children, on their return, realized that something had happened, and that the atmosphere of the house was charged with unknown forces. Things were somehow different, and they unconsciously tried to locate the new centre of gravity. Little Edith was the first to light on a clue, and she exclaimed :

" Why, Auntie, what has happened ? The lines have all gone from your forehead."

" I have spent this afternoon with the Lord Jesus and He has made me so happy," was Miss Soltau's reply.

" Has Jesus been here and we missed Him ? " said one very small child.

At this point Lydia kissed them all and asked them to forgive her bad tempers. The children did not understand what it was all about, but quick, childish sympathy helped them to feel that something wonderful had taken place.

Such an experience as that through which Miss Soltau had just passed caused every nerve and fibre of her being to respond to the vibration of the life force which now possessed her, and was renewing her physical frame more than she at the moment realized. The routine of the day's work was lightened by a sense of increased capacity—capacity for work, for enjoyment, for emotion, for delight in service, in brief, life in abundance, overflowing and breaking down the limits of its former channels.

The following Sunday morning she broke bread with the Brethren, as her custom was. At midday Lydia, anxious to have her share in this new spiritual manifestation, begged that Miss Soltau would come to the Bible Class of which she was a member. Miss Soltau consented, and the bath-chair was soon brought to the door.

To anyone familiar with the hilly surroundings of Hastings it may not be surprising to hear that when the man found he was required to draw Miss Soltau to the summit of the steepest hill backing the town, he firmly refused to entertain the proposal.

"If you paid me ever so, Miss, I would not do it, no, not for no money."

The crestfallen Lydia urged him to make an effort, but in vain.

"No, my dear," he repeated, "never."

Miss Soltau deliberated and made a sudden resolution.

"Lydia," she said, "I will walk."

Had she declared she would fly, the effect could not have been more startling, for she had never yet walked up the hill during her residence in Hastings, and Lydia, though prepared for the day of miracles, thought this was going a little too far.

"It ain't no good, Miss, yer ain't able for it. I'll 'ave yer dead on me 'ands."

Miss Soltau, however, felt that this was a venture calling for a manifestation of faith, and, with her mind fixed on the story of Peter's venture on the water, she sallied forth. Like Peter, she was once nearly overwhelmed, but she reached the top of the hill.

Facing a room full of young women she thought she must collapse, so great had been the physical effort and mental tension. When the time came for her to speak she was able to do so, and with such power that the girls were in tears around her as she described her experiences. For two hours she held their attention and one after another yielded her life to Christ.

" When I came out of that room," she records " I felt like a bird released from a cage. The air was lovely, and I walked down the hill rejoicing in new life."

V

HENRIETTA SOLTAU'S cousin, Mrs. Cecil Bewes, still lived near Plymouth. She was a confirmed invalid and seldom left her room, but her daughters were among the most energetic workers at D. L. Moody's campaign in the West of England. When he himself left Devonshire, these Christian people carried forward the work into villages and hamlets, feeling it incumbent on them to share the ingathering of a harvest which his visit had proved to be ripe.

Prayer meetings, cottage meetings and evangelistic services were held, and as spring advanced and the busy farming season drew near, a large public Hall was hired for one final gathering before the unavoidable break of the summer.

There was much to do in connection with the meeting and Georgie Bewes was inspired to write and ask her cousin Henrietta to come and help. Miss Soltau was most desirous of accepting the invitation, for her own hope was that she might communicate to her invalid cousin the spiritual vigour which had renewed her own physical strength. A Hastings friend offered to take charge of the children and set her free, so joyfully she left for Plymouth.

On arrival she had the great disappointment of finding that her cousin would not respond and claim the healing of her body. Being quite convinced that sofa life was the will of God for her, she accepted it with cheerful resignation. Henrietta therefore turned her energies in other directions and, with her cousin Georgie as companion, drove round the district in a trap, distributing tracts, holding cottage meetings, and listening with delight to the testimonies given by many who had lately escaped from the City of Destruction and started on the heavenly pilgrimage.

The public meeting was widely advertised and at the hour appointed crowds filled the Hall. It was to be addressed by one of the leading Brethren from the Plymouth meeting. Miss Bewes presided at the piano and led the choir which was formed of a number of enthusiastic helpers.

Miss Soltau writes: " Time went by, but the speaker of the evening failed to appear. We were all together in the Hall, but still the preacher did not come and, though no one knew exactly what had happened, it was evident that he must have missed the train. We sang hymn after hymn while a cousin tried to induce one of the workers to throw himself into the breach, but no one would do it. The gallery filled up with rough lads from the mines, who quickly grasped the situation and freely chaffed the promoters of the meeting. They

were quick to see the subterfuges used to prolong
the preliminaries and observed the failure of Miss
Bewes to coax anyone on to the platform.

" ' Let's 'ave another hymn, Miss ! ' they shouted.
' Where's the preacher ? ' ' Ain't it time to close,
my dear ? ' And watching Miss Bewes, slightly
agitated, move from one person to another, ' 'Ee's
no go, Miss ! ' they called out.

" I saw that something must be done and suggested to my cousin that she should give her
testimony. She hesitated a moment because her
father was there, but then she rose and came
forward. As she did so, a hush fell on the restless
congregation. She testified in a simple, telling way,
to the fresh revelation which had come to her
from Mr. Moody's meetings. This occupied but
a few moments, and then we had to fall back on
another hymn. There was still no speaker, but the
audience was quieter and she whispered to me :
' Now you speak.' I trembled for a moment and
in my heart prayed to God for a message. Instantly
there flashed into my mind the words of Isaiah :
' Let the wicked forsake his way and the unrighteous man his thoughts, and let him return
unto the Lord and He will have mercy upon him,
and to our God, for He will abundantly pardon.'

" I stepped forward, and fixing my eyes on the
lads in the gallery gave out my text. I spoke, and
as I did so the Spirit of God fell on the crowded

congregation and many wept. The ringleader of the rough crew buried his head in his folded arms. An outburst of prayer followed my address and cries for salvation were heard. I asked my cousin to keep the congregation singing appropriate hymns while we moved among the audience and spoke to those who were anxious. I had led six to Christ before I reached the gallery stairs. I heard groans from thence. All helpers were busy, and even timid cousins who had been unwilling to speak were dealing with souls under conviction of sin. At last I reached the lad in the gallery, but not till eleven p.m. did light break upon his soul. He was gloriously saved. That Thursday evening was a night to be remembered. The Lord had set me free to be His witness.

" Two days later I saw this lad Robert standing in the hall of my cousin's house with his arm in a sling, and, running down stairs, I heard him say :

" ' The doctor says I must take the next train home to my mother. Her lives at Ivybridge. I may have the lock-jaw in twenty-four hours but seems to me, lady, the Lord who 'ealed my soul that 'ere Thursday night could just the same 'eal my 'and. We was blasting rock in the quarry, Miss, and a great block fell and crushed my 'and and 'eld me there. I did not swear. I just called out, " Praise the Lord." When my mates heard that, they was frightened and said : " Robert, you'll die." (I used to swear awful before I was saved.) I said, " Well, mates, if I die, I'll go straight to heaven." The Lord saved my soul Thursday and I bain't afraid to die. They took me to the doctor. The blood was running fast, and he said, " You'll never use that 'and again," but, lady, don't you think the Lord can 'eal my 'and as easily as He did my soul ? I could not sleep for joy after the Lord washed my 'eart clean. I got a Bible last night from a neighbour and I opened it at the Actees. I read the story of that 'ere man who had never walked and Peter and John 'ealed him. It was the Name of Jesus. Can't He 'eal me, Miss ? '

" ' Yes, Robert,' I replied, ' let us kneel down and trust Him.'

" He poured out his heart in prayer in such broad Devonshire dialect, that I do not know how to write it. When we arose he said :

" ' I do not think, lady, I will go home to-night. To-morrow be Sunday. B'ain't you going to speak to the lads ? '

" ' Yes,' I said, ' at three o'clock.'

" ' Then I'll be there. Can't I go somewhere in the morning ? Where do you go, Miss ? '

" ' I am going to a hall in Ridgeway,' I said.

" ' Then I'll come too,' said Robert.

" Again in the afternoon he was there. The kitchen was filled with village lads and another room with girls. The Holy Spirit worked mightily and many came to Christ.

"As I returned to Hastings on Monday Robert came with me as far as Ivybridge, full of joy, to tell his mother of his new-found Saviour. That day week he was back in the quarry using the right hand which was perfectly whole. From this time onwards I unhesitatingly accepted invitations to preach in the villages around Hastings."

VI

EVERY form of human suffering made direct
appeal to Henrietta Soltau's compassion, and
she observed how the solid comfort demanded
by the fashionable *clientèle* of Hastings required
the service of an army of drudges to sustain its
standard. In dark basements young servant girls
spent their days in ceaseless toil, climbing exhausted
to their attics at night to snatch what sleep they
could during the insufficient hours allowed them.
Wearied by the perpetual answering of bells
which summoned them up two or three flights
of stairs for some trivial service, their tempers
became short and their characters warped. The
title of 'slavey' was an appropriate one. During
busy seasons a begrudged afternoon out on
alternate Sundays, was the sum total of their
recreation.

No one cared for their welfare until the
Wellington Square band of pray-ers realized a
debt toward them. How to reach this class was
a difficult problem, for any approach to the houses
where they lived would be fiercely resented by
the lodging-house keepers, and it was questionable
if an ordinary meeting would present any attraction
to them. An invitation to tea was clearly the way

to meet the situation and before long, one hundred
and forty invitations were sent out.

On the day fixed, seventy little maids-of-all-
work arrived, and were received, welcomed and
waited on with kindly courtesy by the hostesses.
After tea one of the travelling secretaries of
the Y.W.C.A. spoke to them. She was young,
good-looking, well-dressed and her manners were
charming. Her purpose was quite definite—
to offer salvation in Christ's name to these
girls whom she might never see again. Some
responded, many went away deeply impressed,
and to all the thought of an occasional gathering
of this kind was a bright hope in the monotony
of existence.

In business houses the demands on the assistants
were scarcely less exacting. Long hours of standing,
poor food and poor sleeping accommodation, kept
them anaemic, weary and jaded. There was little
for them in the life of the churches, whose regular
services were made to suit the leisured. The
recently organized movement, known as the Young
Women's Christian Association, which cared for
such girls, was growing rapidly and extending its
activities to all the important towns. Henrietta
Soltau and her comrades felt the time had come to
go forward and establish a branch in Hastings,
but this was a costly business, requiring outlay
on a very different scale from that needed for a

friendly cup of tea and the travelling expenses of
a speaker from Brighton.

Many employers and heads of departments
welcomed an effort which was clearly for the
good of their employees and encouraged the
suggestion. A hall was hired for the sum of one
guinea and the result of the first meeting was so
encouraging that it was decided to carry on a
weekly gathering of the same character for as long
as funds would permit. The money required
was supplied for a whole year by various friends
and at the end of this time Henrietta Soltau, in
conjunction with her friends, Charlotte and Emily
Murray, determined to launch out and take a house
to be known as the Y.W.C.A. Institute.

There was a suitable place in Wellington Square.
The rent was one hundred and twenty pounds
per annum and they offered eighty pounds for
immediate possession. The offer was accepted
and the ladies found themselves tenants of a large
empty house with nothing in hand for furnishing.

Little Lucy threw herself into the breach with
five shillings, her sole worldly possessions, and
went with Miss Soltau to a second-hand furniture
shop where a nice little book-case was purchased
for this exact sum and proudly conveyed to
number thirty-seven. It was a small beginning,
but an earnest of things to come, and a donation
of two hundred pounds from a friend at Eastbourne

swept them into the house on a wave of prosperity. There was space to accommodate thirty boarders, and the rooms were simply furnished for the sum of one hundred pounds plus Lucy's five shillings. This Institute and Holiday Home has been a centre of blessing ever since.

By this time Miss Soltau was well known in Hastings as one to whom those in need might turn for help. As she was travelling one day in the omnibus, a conductor turned and spoke to her :

" Excuse me, Miss, but why is it the chaps on the Railway has special meetings and the busmen has none ? "

" The Sunday meeting is open to everyone," she answered.

" Sunday is no holiday to the busman, Miss."

This was an opening, and after talking it over with her friends, she decided to invite all the men in the employ of the Omnibus Company to a tea, to be followed by an evangelistic service. The children helped to decorate the room, tables were laid and there was good food in abundance, but the guests did not turn up. The converted carpenter, whose services were essential to such an occasion, was most indignant that his lady should receive such a rebuff. She, however, was quite equal to the occasion and resorted to the Scriptural method of compelling guests to her feast.

All the available helpers were sent out to invite any who were willing to come, and the room was soon filled with a miscellaneous company, a pathetic crowd of derelicts, homeless, friendless and hungry in a town given up to merry-making. They did full justice to the busmen's good tea and when the meal was over there was a general move to leave, but it was found that all doors were locked and were not to be opened until the Gospel service was over. The young curate chose the fifty-third chapter of Isaiah for his text, but the more experienced hostess followed on with the story of the marriage-feast, an easy illustration being ready to hand.

On enquiry it was found that none of the busmen had been free at the hour fixed for the tea, and that the only suitable time for them was midnight. Miss Soltau, not to be outdone, arranged a midnight tea from which not one man was absent. These gatherings also were held regularly, and later on a special evangelistic mission for men was conducted by Dr. Harry Guinness, at which scores were converted.

After occupying a small and dark house at the corner of the Square for several years Miss Soltau was able to move her family to more suitable premises. A friend of her brother George came to see her, and, commented on the lack of space for the children. " They ought to have more light and space, Miss Soltau," he began. "George has done so much for my boys that I should like to make some return to his sister. While I am in Hastings I shall call on some agents and see what can be done."

In a few days he was back again with the news of a good house in the immediate neighbourhood at a rental of fifty pounds.

"Do not be anxious about the rent," he said, "I shall give you thirty pounds a year towards it, so that your expenses will not be increased."

With great delight they inspected the new premises which were airy, spacious, and had a nice outlook. The large drawing-room would be very suitable for meetings, and on the following quarter-day Miss Soltau and the children moved in amid great rejoicing.

The next year the kind donor died after the payment of but one instalment of thirty pounds, and the house which had promised to be such a blessing, became a heavy weight on Miss Soltau's hands. When the first quarter's rent became due she was still ten pounds short of the amount needed. Beset with questionings and doubts she wondered if she had been right in incurring the extra expense when the smaller house, though not suitable, had been possible.

"The rent is high," she wrote to her brother, "and expenses are in every way heavier than they were in my little dark corner. Hitherto the use made of the house seems too small to warrant the increased outlay. . . . Moreover again and again there comes such an overpowering desire upon me to be out on the mission field, that I feel it is not restlessness but the stirring of the Holy Spirit."

A few anxious, sleepless nights soon brought back distressing headaches, and she suddenly seemed wholly unfitted for all the responsibilities she had taken on herself. For the time being her mind ceased to be garrisoned with the peace of God, and the trial of her faith reached a climax when the house agent called in person for the rent which she was not able to produce.

With one cry of distress she looked up to her God and her prayer was a groan that could not be uttered. At that very moment a knock at the front door announced a visitor and Miss Soltau, outwardly calm, went forward to greet a young lady whose face she had noticed at the Y.W.C.A. meetings, but to whom she had never spoken. In a simple and well-bred way the caller explained her errand.

"It is a matter of some delicacy," she said. "My aged father insists that I should bring you, from him, a present of money to be used in whatever way it may be needed in your work. I have it here in a handkerchief, just as he tied it up himself. Please excuse this unconventional way of handing it over." Still speaking, she emptied on to the table fifteen golden sovereigns. God had sent the rent, and by the hand of one who was to become Henrietta Soltau's life-long friend.

Without explanation she took the money, excused herself, paid the agent and came back to talk with her guest. In later years the two women often laughed over this incident. Her friend had believed herself to be calling on a lady of considerable means and could find no excuse for offering her a present of fifteen pounds.

VII

ONE great event of this period, for Henrietta, was the return to England of her brother Henry, who had succeeded in accomplishing the pioneer journey through Burma into Yünnan across China with J. W. Stevenson. Great things had happened.

The two men had been received by aboriginal tribes. A chieftain's wife had been dangerously ill, and the missionaries had been called to her assistance. The tribes-people seeing her cured opened their hearts and homes to the miracle-working evangelists and, when the time came, led them through unknown mountain-passes to the border of China.

Henry Soltau was brimful of information regarding a fascinating and little-known people, and hoped to secure recruits for their evangelization. During the time he spent in Hastings he aroused much missionary enthusiasm, but none of his hearers were more thrilled than the 'Juvenile Missionary Band,' led by his sister, which now numbered fifty members and held its meetings in a small hall. Henry Soltau had a gift for speaking to children and they were entranced as he graphically described to them the sorrows of children in heathen lands, how they bowed down to idols of wood and stone and knew nothing of God, or Jesus Christ the Saviour.

At the close of their meeting, the children of Henrietta's household returned home in a subdued mood and were later discovered in small groups conferring on some important matter.

Lydia came to Miss Soltau to report suspicious doings in the nursery.

" If you please, ma'am, them children has some sort of a plan on foot."

" Nothing wrong, I hope, Lydia," said Miss Soltau.

" I didn't say it was nothing wrong, Miss, but they's all crying about their dolls 'aving to go to Burma."

Miss Soltau went down to the playroom and found the children with tear-stained faces, each hugging a doll.

" What is this, my dears ? " she asked.

" Uncle Henry will have to take our dolls back to Burma with him," said Edie.

" The children there have no toys to play with," said Lucy, "and no one to tell them about Jesus."

Their treasured dolls were so battered and shabby and their playthings at all times so few that Miss Soltau deferred the discussion till next day.

" It is nine o'clock, children, time you were all in bed," she said. ". Now don't keep Lydia waiting, and I will come up and say good-night when you are ready."

Half an hour later, as she went round to tuck up the little cots, she noticed that each child had her doll by her under the bed-clothes, but she made no comment. Next morning she realized the full import of the unusual proceeding for, on her study sofa, she found a row of shabby dolls and pinned to each a slip of paper on which was written in a large childish hand some such inscription as : ' God is love.' ' Jesus wept.' ' Good-bye, my darling Rosie.' ' With love and kisses from Edie.' Such an offering of love could not be refused, although its disposal was somewhat embarrassing.

" You must get the dolls to Burma," she said to her brother, " this offering has cost the children too much for their sacrifice not to be accepted."

The children cried most of the day after their dolls were gone, and while Henry Soltau was packing them for Burma, as he conscientiously did, he meditated on the blessedness and privilege of sacrifice which begins with giving a toy and ends by giving a life.

For several months there was a blank in the children's lives, blue-eyed Rosie, pink-cheeked

Ruby, smiling black Toby were on their way to Burma and their loving little mothers would never see them again. Miss Soltau would gladly have given each child a new doll, but felt the incident was too sacred for her to interfere; so doll-less they remained until Christmas Eve. On that night a box arrived containing one boy and one girl doll for each child. On Christmas morning when they saw the new toys they jumped and clapped their hands for joy, but though they treasured their new playthings, these never filled the places of those which had gone to Burma.

The Monday afternoon prayer-meeting already referred to, continued to be well attended. Its members, though intensely in earnest, were baffled, perplexed and felt helpless in the face of the fashionable and other crowds which frequented Hastings. Prayer, however, could not be unavailing and Hastings soon began to feel its impact. The first aggressive effort was a successful beach mission for children which lasted through four weeks of unbroken fine weather and bore a harvest of conversions among visitors' children.

In those days open-air meetings met with lively opposition, and even the Children's Missioner experienced difficulty. Hired roughs threw stones and crackers freely among the children to frighten them, but the services went on in spite of them, and when the beach services closed down, the Salvation Army continued the attack. The large Music Hall was hired for the opening of the campaign, which was conducted by Catherine Booth. Her words roused multitudes to feel the emptiness and uselessness of their lives, and many came to the penitent form. Salvation Army processions were attacked by the Skeleton Army, inspired, organized and financed by the local publicans, but, as in other places, the skeletons returned to their graves while the Salvation Army marched on.

In 1884 Henrietta Soltau was asked to be temporarily responsible for the Sunday evening meetings at the Railway Mission Hall. These, she knew, would bring her into more direct contact with men and women whom she might win for Christ. There she quite simply followed the leadings of the Spirit and God set His seal upon her labours, for every service saw men and women yielding to Christ and every week the attendance grew.

She had the full sympathy of her brother George in reaching this decision, as his views on the ministry of women had also been completely revolutionized. He had seen the blessing of God resting upon the work of his gifted wife, and wrote to his sister: " I want Grace to start a Sunday afternoon meeting at which she shall take up many of the important points of our modern spurious Christianity, somewhat on the lines of Mrs. Booth. I have a strong impression that she may draw the men whom no Church will attract. I have been much blessed in reading Mrs. Booth's life. It has been a strong tonic to my soul."

Only ten of the Railway men were definitely Christian, but there were a dozen more who attended the services more or less regularly. The problem was how to draw in the godless men who were in an overwhelming majority at the station. She had an enthusiastic co-worker in an engine driver who was converted through reading books written by her father and who was not afraid of rebuff.

Numbers crept up but slowly until one evening she boldly called on the converted men present to bear testimony to their companions. From that night blessing began, and she felt that at last she had the clue as to how best to get at the men. By the end of three months sixty men attended regularly, the large majority of them having experienced personal conversion during that period. She and her colleagues then waxed bolder and arranged a tea-meeting to which the Christian men brought eighty of their roughest and most godless companions, including some notorious characters. The fun, laughter and jokes at the

tea-table were disconcerting to the ladies presiding
at the urns, whose whole concern was for the
success of the evangelistic address to follow. The
meeting began in a spirit of exhilaration and the
two women evangelists who had specially come
from Brighton were received with clapping, cheering and loud encouragement. Luckily they were
equal to the occasion and provoked applause by
introducing themselves as the 'Engine' and the
'Tender.' Before they had finished they had
hit out so hard that the deep hush was broken
only by the sobs of those under conviction of
sin.

At the close several men bolted for the door,
but Henrietta was a match for them and they
found her waiting in the lobby to net them. Soon
the Railway Mission came to be one of the most
important evangelistic agencies in Hastings.

The children were by no means sleeping partners
in this work, and every Sunday evening paid a
round of visits on their way to the service for the
purpose of inviting special friends to join them.
One of them writes :

" We children hailed this new branch of work
with great joy, as we were allowed to attend the
Sunday evening services which were then held
in the Parish Schoolroom, where we sat on the
top of the infants' desks and enjoyed the singing
and the addresses. Whenever we travelled to

London we always went to see if a friend were driving the train. Then we found out the guards, porters and platelayers whom we knew."

Another great favourite was the carpenter who often came to the house for odd jobs. The boys delighted in his clever ways with tools, and he was good-natured in allowing them to help. It had, however, been brought to their notice through Miss Soltau's prayers that he was 'an infidel,' which term conveyed to their minds that he did not love God. Mary had on one occasion boldly cross-questioned him as to this mysterious attitude of mind, and came back to the others with the information that his answer was :

"Don't you trouble your head about that little Miss, or Miss Soltau will be angry. I have no time to be running round to meetings."

"You will have to be converted," was her answer, "because Miss Soltau prays for you every day." "Then," she said, "he just grunted."

This manner of closing the interview had some how shown her that his opinion on the subject was different from that held by Miss Soltau. The children were allowed to give him one of the Christmas puddings so miraculously supplied, and the first visit they paid to his home was to present it. Now that they knew where he lived they arranged to call for him on their way to the Sunday evening meeting at the Railway Mission, and he found himself quite unable to refuse their childish entreaties. One Sunday evening One met him there Whose pleadings he found it still less possible to resist, and the infidel carpenter became a disciple of the Carpenter of Nazareth.

VIII

"OUR position to one another in our families is, and must be, like that of the moon to the earth. The moon revolves round her, moves with her, never leaves her, yet the earth never sees but one side of her, the other side remains for ever unknown." A woman of that period, one who was both good and wise, wrote these significant words, and Henrietta, though in the happy position of being member of a family which in spiritual matters presented a united front, often had cause to realize the truth of this statement. She suffered considerable misunderstanding in regard to her method of life from her mother, to whom it was easier to be proud of a son, pioneering in a remote country, than of a daughter who was an active Christian propagandist in a fashionable watering-place. To see Ettie throw physical limitations to the wind, and undertake heavy financial responsibilities with no visible means of support, was a sore trial, and her sense of social fitness was constantly outraged. There was, moreover, in their intercourse a shade of resentment that a child who, according to Victorian ideas, should have no secrets from a parent, managed her house without reference to her mother although she was living close at hand.

That tramps and busmen should be looked after was as it should be, and could lead to no possible social embarrassment, but there was something in the expression of Henrietta's human relationships with all and sundry which was most disconcerting. Mrs. Soltau never knew whom she might find in her daughter's drawing-room and there were occasionally awkward moments for all concerned. Then, there was the matter of dress. Mrs. Soltau would have been horrified had one of her daughters appeared in over-fashionable clothes, but it annoyed her seriously to see Henrietta enter her house in garments which, though always scrupulously neat, might be mended, darned or shabby as necessity demanded—clothes which, in a word, she regarded as unfit for a lady of her social upbringing.

Yet under the peculiar circumstances of Henrietta's life, she held herself under obligation to meet all liabilities of her household before thinking of her clothes. It was not for her to question the method of God's provision for her needs. She lived from hand to mouth, but it was God's hand and her mouth. So throughout her life she regarded every penny which passed through her hands as a sacred trust.

One spring the sunshine was revealing the shabbiness of a bonnet which had done service for too many months, and Henrietta shrank from the scrutiny of her mother's critical eye on

it. Nor did it make her more comfortable when
Mrs. Soltau handed her some money which was
due to her, saying in a peremptory tone :

"Take this, Ettie, and remember you have no
excuse now for not buying yourself a new bonnet.
Do go at once and get a really nice one for
Sunday. Give the one you have on to your
charwoman."

Henrietta realized that quarter-day was at hand
and that five pounds were still needed to meet
the rent. Knowing that she could not promise to
spend the money on dress she made use of the
well-known subterfuge with which she, as a
child, had often been bluffed by her elders, and
merely answered :

"I will see."

"Don't see ; go and buy it at once," was the
sharp answer.

Henrietta went home, thought over it, prayed
over it, and deliberately used the whole amount
for payment of the rent. She was glad indeed to
take advantage of an excuse which prevented
her seeing her mother for a few days. On the
third morning the postman delivered a bandbox
holding, she says, " the prettiest little bonnet I
had ever seen, sent to me by a friend who was
compelled to go into mourning." With a light
heart she put it on and went to pay her mother
a visit.

"That is right, Ettie, I am glad to see that for once you have listened to advice. At last you have a bonnet which is both pretty and ladylike."

With her brothers and sisters, scattered in various countries, she was able to keep up a semblance of intimacy. On matters of spiritual experience she was expressive, in recording incidents of daily life she was exemplary, in editing a family budget she was punctilious ; she shared with them the joys and sorrows of her work in Hastings as well as the interests of their own varied lives, but throughout the voluminous correspondence not one sentence can be found naked enough to reveal the real woman.

Her mother would have been amazed had she seen the letters to the children's parents, which reveal how deeply she was occasionally wounded by misunderstanding. The position which she held was liable at any time to provoke jealousy on the part of father or mother from whom the children had to be separated for such long periods during their most impressionable and dependent years. They *must* turn to someone with their childish confidences, and the person who would most naturally receive them was their faithful guardian and friend Henrietta Soltau. Although she loyally guarded the position of father and mother in the child's heart and mind, never allowing herself by word or act to usurp that which was due to another, it is not surprising that on more than one occasion she found the atmosphere to be suddenly electric.

The sacrifice made by the missionary parent is one too great for any outsider to gauge, and the problem of providing for children during those difficult years of separation almost impossible of solution. Her difficulty was how to fill the place without taking the place. While in many cases she met with nothing but appreciation, she sometimes received letters, or sat through interviews, which sent her on her way with a sick and aching heart.

Extracts from correspondence will best show how hard was the work which she had undertaken and how thankless at times :

" It is very long since I have had a line from you, sometimes I wonder if you are ever going to write again. I so much want to know your wishes regarding your child and whether it is your desire that she should visit your relatives in X——. They are most anxious to have her, but since your last remarks I do not feel free to let her go without your consent. . . ."

" I have continued Muriel's music and French lessons all the year and she has made good progress in both. I do not know if I can continue them further, for I have had more than ordinary trials of faith this year. I have often hoped that the

Lord would guide and enable you to sometimes send me help for her board. . . ."

" I am very thankful to tell you that last year I was able to meet all fees, the Lord having enabled me to do this in an unexpected manner, but I cannot promise to undertake further this heavy expense. My little fund will be completely exhausted when I have paid the two children's school-bills. Seeing that you now have some prospect before you, I feel it right to tell you how I am circumstanced. You know I draw no funds from the China Inland Mission and am entirely dependent on what parents are able to send or on what Christian friends may supply from time to time. All that I possess I willingly give and have given to this work. I cannot do more and expenses are heavy. I have had some sharp trials this year and feel there may be more coming. I have drawn all my own property out now and have nothing more to lay on the altar. I did not wish to write on this matter. . . ."

" It seems as if our letters for sever l months past have been at cross-purposes and misunderstandings. I have only tried to answer your repeated questions concerning Leonard's expenses. I should not have referred to them had you not asked again and again. I gathered from your letters that you preferred his being with his relations. I am certainly pained at many of the matters referred to in your last letter. I should not have wondered so much had you not been so lately in England and had your child with you for so long. . . . You surely know enough of our home life to realize the perfect freedom and happiness of the children and of their affection one for another and, thank God, for me. Had you not been satisfied about this you surely would not have left him here again and asked me to care for Nora also. . . ."

As we have already observed, the parents of the children were located in various countries and in remote parts of the world. From time to time Miss Soltau received from some of them, in lieu of remittances, presents of articles which were both valuable and rare. While acknowledging with gratitude the affection these gifts expressed she felt that in view of more urgent needs, she must ask them to desist or allow her to sell the goods for the benefit of the children.

" Will you bear with me, dear Mrs. K., in saying that our love and friendship for one another does not need the expression of costly gifts, and while we are fellow-labourers in the service of one Lord and Master do not burden yourself to send me these valuable things. Will you understand me when I say that I have found, since I yielded myself to the Lord for the service of caring for your children and others, that I must deny myself the pleasure

of giving, as I used to do, love-tokens to loving
friends. My one anxiety is to provide things honest
in the sight of all men and to meet the many
increasing demands of this work. Each year's
growth of the dear children brings the need of
increased outlay. Of the presents which I have
hitherto received I never hesitate to sell any,
where a good price is offered. This last week I
sold the last three pieces I had left and a lady begged
for a pair of my blue ringed cups, so I let them go
as I was glad of the money for the children's
summer clothes. They are a pair you sent me
four years ago and have held flowers constantly
ever since."

Thus she moved amidst a wide circle, every
member of which saw a different facet of her
character. To her mother she was the devoted
but somewhat erratic daughter, earnest but over-
zealous, and regrettably unwilling to benefit by
the experience of those who had been longer in
the world than herself. To other members of her
family she was the beloved sister whose devotion
to the Lord was an example and inspiration. In
Brethren circles she was appreciated as being the
worthy daughter of an illustrious man, as well
as for her personal goodness, but open to a measure
of censure for the unauthorised liberty of action
which she claimed as her right. To the busmen,
railwaymen and others, she was the ideal of woman-

hood, ever ready with encouragement and practical help. Among the children she was gay and debonair, and their simplicity set her free of customary restraints.

In all the wide circle her only close friendship was with Adeline Braithwaite, who in 1883 wintered in Hastings with her father. A spiritual comradeship was established between the two women and they fostered a hope of working together in China which hope, however, was never realized, for Adeline Braithwaite married Walter Campbell and accompanied him on his evangelistic tours in the East while Henrietta's life-work tied her to London.

Henrietta Soltau was a friend to many but her intimacies were few. She had the remoteness of those who give liberally and receive sparingly. Her wide-open front door made her accessible to all and the uniform cordiality of her reception established an easy atmosphere of friendliness, but the aura which she diffused was more light than warmth, more the brilliance of a gem-like flame than the heat of a passionate soul.

IX

HENRIETTA SOLTAU lived for nine years
in Hastings, holding herself ready for any
manner of service that God might require of her,
and every kind of evangelistic activity seemed
to grow up around her. The Y.W.C.A. thrived;
the Railway Mission had become a centre of
evangelism for working men and their families;
midnight meetings for busmen were held regularly;
the homeless tramps were not forgotten, and the
little maids-of-all-work for whom no one else
cared, looked forward to their Quarterly Social.
Two missionary working-parties met at her house,
when information direct from the field was circu-
lated and stirred many hearts to gifts and service;
but, above all, the weekly prayer-meeting, held
in her drawing-room, became the power house
from which potent spiritual forces were distributed
to distant outposts.

Apart from these regular interests Miss Soltau's
freedom from family, professional or business
claims brought around her a large number of men
and women needing help, advice or sympathy.
She was always accessible and anyone might come
to her irrespective of all social conventionalities.
It was true of her as of a modern woman preacher

" She is one of the few busy people who always convey to her visitors a sense of leisure and appreciation that they have permitted her to be of service to them." Her spiritual alertness kept her always on the watch for an opportunity to impart. No case seemed to her hopeless, so that many despairing people left her sitting-room renewed in hope.

To the members of her own circle it seemed as though God had appointed her life-work in Hastings, but she and her friend, Miss Braithwaite, alone knew that they often met to pray that if it were the will of God, they might yet go out to the Far East as working members of the China Inland Mission.

Her improved physical condition warranted her entertaining this hope and she wrote to her intimate friend : " I have a strange though definite consciousness that God is calling me to a fresh path of service and is loosening all the bonds that are holding me to this place. I feel impelled to tell you this. I have no guidance. I may be busy with just the same work as has grown up around me during these eight years, but a voice sounds again and again within me saying, ' Arise ye and depart, for this is not your rest.' To that voice I cannot but reply, ' Here am I, Lord, send me.' I do not see any immediate step to be taken, but God is surely preparing me for something, though what that may be I cannot say."

Thus matters stood in May, 1889, when a telegram came from Dr. Hudson Taylor asking her to meet him in London to confer on an important matter. Miss Braithwaite was with her and the two friends went together to the house of Mr. and Mrs. Broomhall, in Pyrland Road, Mildmay, where the business of the China Inland Mission was conducted.

It was a very vital time in the history of the Mission, and No. 2 Pyrland Road was all too small for the numbers coming and going. In 1887 one hundred new workers had sailed for China and in the course of the following year seventy more had left England. All the candidates either stayed in Mrs. Broomhall's house, or in lodgings close at hand, and Mrs. Broomhall herself was completely overstrained by the magnitude of the work required of her.

Dr. Hudson Taylor saw that the hour had come for extending the work of the home department by opening a house to be used for the reception and testing of women candidates, and it was to ask Miss Soltau to undertake the oversight of this department that he had sent for her. As he unfolded his plan and she listened to what he had to say, every kind of difficulty loomed large in her mind. How could she handle candidates for a foreign field which she had never even seen? Also she did not feel strong enough for life in a London suburb. Was it reasonable to suppose that God would ask her to lay down the care of the children for which she felt she was fitted, and take up a career for which she knew her own training to be inadequate?

She spoke little, but listened to all he had to say, then travelled back to Hastings under strong conviction that to accept his offer would be a grievous mistake.

In the days which followed, as she constantly turned the matter over in her mind, she could see no way of complying with the request, and yet she could not deny that Dr. Hudson Taylor's complete conviction that she was the one chosen of God to fill the post, was disconcerting, so she made her prayer to God that were this appointment truly of Him, He would Himself set her at liberty for the new work, by taking away the children from her care. Of the problem which faced her she resolved to say nothing to the group of her Hastings friends.

Her little family was at this time representative of four Continents, Asia, Africa, Southern Europe and Australia, and she had every reason to believe that the present group would need her care for some years to come, even if she admitted no new inmates to the household.

Within a few weeks a startling communication reached her. The mother of two children wrote from China that she and her husband were taking unexpected furlough and wished to remove their children by the following September. Close on this came a letter from a parent in North Africa saying that a free passage was offered for all his children to join him in Morocco. Preparations had to be hastily set on foot and the children were outfitted and dispatched at an early date. Yet one more parent wrote that he wanted his children in Australia, as soon as a suitable escort was available. No sooner had they sailed than a letter came from Spain which resulted in two more of the rapidly dwindling family leaving her. She was almost frightened to see the hand of God turning her into the path she wished to avoid.

With characteristic reticence about her own affairs, Miss Soltau had told none of her friends what the scattering of the children would mean for her, and when, finally, she made known to the inner circle what Dr. Hudson Taylor was asking of her, and that she would probably be leaving Hastings, there was a storm of protest.

Various members of her family strongly disapproved and considered the plan unwise, from every point of view. One of her best friends spoke plainly :

" The selection of candidates requires a peculiar gift of insight and discernment of character which you obviously do not possess."

She could but agree.

The wider circle of her acquaintance was convinced that she would be making the greatest mistake of her life.

" What about all the evangelistic activities that you have set in motion ? It is impossible for you to leave them."

The confusion arising from such a multitude of counsellors baffled and distressed her spirit, and to one and all she could but answer : " One door has closed behind me, my children have been scattered, I have no option but to enter the open door before me."

By the month of November her happy home was broken up. Every child had been withdrawn from her care ; she moved to North London, and Wellington Square knew her no more.

THE HEAT OF THE DAY

I

DR. HUDSON TAYLOR had taken 41 and 41A
Pyrland Road as headquarters for the Women
Candidates' department, and Miss Soltau found
herself forthwith in possession of two typical
North London houses. The situation was healthy
and not overcrowded, but the unutterable dreariness
of the northern suburb lay like a pall on her spirit.
The variety and brightness of a sea-side town gave
place to monotonous rows of houses which it
seemed impossible to distinguish one from another.

The dining-room, large and bare, was scantily
furnished with a long dining-table surrounded by
bent-wood chairs which, standing unoccupied,
only served for the moment to emphasize the
emptiness of the house. A second large room was
set apart as students' study. It held another long
table, more bent-wood chairs and a blackboard.

A dingy garden boasted some smutty shrubs,
and constant trains ran past on their journey between
Mildmay Park and Canonbury stations. The
surroundings could scarcely have been more gloomy,
and as Miss Soltau sat there, waiting for the arrival
of the first candidate, her loneliness knew no
bounds. She had no idea how to begin with that
young woman, how to prepare her for what lay

ahead, or even how to judge of her fitness for missionary life.

At Dr. Taylor's express desire the home was financed from the funds of the Mission, and her house accounts were to be periodically submitted to the Treasurer. The general control of the home was to some extent in the hands of a Women's Council.

It was all so different from the blithe irresponsibility of the Hastings house, where she and the children formed a happy band who fed from their Father's hand, and nostalgia was fed by letters telling her how sorely she was missed. She longed for the children whose presence was a guarantee of joyous gaiety and impromptu pleasures, and in whose company any incident of life might turn into an event of exquisite enjoyment, as also for the happy human intercourse which had converted her sitting-room into a *salon* where she received all who came. Here committees and the routine of institutional life quenched spontaneity, and she was not even free to undertake outside work, for the handling of candidates would probably soon suffice to employ all her energies.

Miss Soltau's own record of her first month in London is that every night she wept tears of loneliness and suffered torments of questioning and doubt as she asked herself, ' Have I made the great mistake of my life? Can it be that the removal of the children was not the act of God to release me, but merely coincidence to test my sense of vocation?' Those who met her day by day, outwardly serene, little knew what exquisite tortures this sensitive soul suffered in the long night-watches.

In January, 1890, the first candidate arrived and after that the house quickly filled. This was the year of Dr. Hudson Taylor's appeal to the Church for a large number of workers to be drafted to China in the course of the next three years. Response came at once from all parts of the British Isles and also from the Continent of Europe, where Mr. Franzen was travelling and stirring missionary interest among the churches.

The China Inland Mission was attracting men and women of strong character, personal devotion and high spiritual development, belonging to all classes of society and many nationalities. The problems arising from differences of upbringing were solved, as to the matter of mutual relationships, by the depth of their common Christian experience and by the sympathy engendered in their common call; but how to discern what particular training each girl needed, presented difficulties which might have baffled a woman of much wider experience.

As the home filled up with enthusiastic young people, bent on preparing themselves in the best

way possible for their life-work, Miss Soltau's
sense of *désœuvrement* vanished, but she was still
troubled by her seeming unfitness for the work.
Her duties included that of acting as secretary to
the Women's Council, and she herself records her
feeling of incapacity as she set herself to the task.
Long hours were spent each day in preparation for
the Bible classes and daily prayers. The continental
candidates had to be taught English. " The preparation of accounts for the Treasurer and Minutes for
the Ladies' Council were my chief burdens."

It was not Dr. Hudson Taylor's purpose that
Miss Soltau should open a Training Home, but
rather that she should receive all and sundry who
were making application to the China Inland
Mission, keep them for a limited period in her
house and seek to form an estimate of their suitability for the work to which they believed themselves to be called. He expected her also to report
on the amount of training necessary in each case.

In this Dr. Taylor showed wisdom. He realized
that the organization of a Candidates' Home and
that of a Training School should differ fundament-
ally. In the former each inmate should be given full
opportunity for freedom of expression so as to
reveal her natural characteristics, whereas in the
Training School necessary discipline should exer-
cise a salutary restraint on idiosyncrasies, its very
rules and regulations inducing a conformity which,

for the time being, must mask individualism. Dr. Taylor's desire was to know his people, and in his opinion no amount of educational training or culture could be compared with the fundamental qualities of sincerity and stability.

Some remarkable women came to 41 Pyrland Road, women who have left a permanent impression upon the Chinese in whose cities they eventually resided. They have, in some cases, been succeeded by workers of much higher educational qualifications and more specialised training, but in knowledge of the Chinese people, mastery of the Chinese language, adaptability to oriental conditions, determination to equip themselves for the work to which they were devoting their lives, and in serious recognition of the mission entrusted to them as ambassadors of the Court of Heaven, these pioneers stand as examples to the present generation.

Henrietta Soltau set her foot on another rung of the ladder of faith during one Saturday afternoon prayer-meeting for China, when mention was made of the inadequate sum in hand for transmission to the field. She had just received from the Treasurer a cheque for household expenses and her heart was burdened as she thought of some lonely workers, perhaps short of necessities, receiving the less because of the sufficient supply of her need. In a moment of illumination she saw the value of her

Hastings experience and she knew herself ready for a severer test.

Instead of cashing the cheque she returned it to the Treasurer. Calling her household together she asked them to join her in prayer that they might all live together the same life of faith that they must be prepared to live when they went to China as members of the Mission. The step was a tremendous one, for large issues were at stake and the lives of many involved, but Henrietta Soltau was a woman who knew her God and could afford to do exploits.

To the whole circle the morning petition, ' Give us this day our daily bread,' came with new force and reality, but the candidates seldom knew how severely her own faith was being tried. " The tests began, but faith strengthened under them and again my spirit was free. With the children I had never spent my last shilling, but now again and again I came to my last penny. Still I held on to the words of Jesus, ' Seek ye first the kingdom of God and His righteousness, and all these things shall be added unto you,' and so they were."

From that day until she resigned control of the Women's Department, she never again needed to fall back on Mission funds for the supply of her household needs.

II

THE China Inland Mission Council had selected the members of a party to sail for China in September, 1890, and Miss Soltau grappled for the first time with the difficulties of outfitting and packing. The hot June days were spent in visiting warehouses and packing tin-lined boxes.

Before the end of the month a letter came from Mrs. Dyce Alexander, inviting her to join one of the house-parties at Keswick for the period of the Convention. "I was tremblingly glad to go to Keswick," writes Miss Soltau. All the spiritual uplift of the last few years had been on the lines of the Keswick teaching, but she knew she might bring herself under criticism by some among Brethren if she attended the Convention, and she also dreaded the crowds.

How could she, as a member of a large house-party, secure the loneliness and quiet necessary to a deep personal spiritual experience? It was in solitude, not in large meetings, that her deepest lessons had been learnt, and she dreaded above all things to hear addresses delivered at Keswick, yet fail to appropriate the messages through lack of direct converse with her Lord. After much searching of heart the invitation was accepted, and she deliberately asked that the sign and earnest of the coming blessing should be that she meet none of her many friends attending that Convention, until such time as the Lord Himself had shown her that for which He had taken her to Keswick.

In telling the story Miss Soltau records as an important factor in her experiences : " Mrs. Alexander gave me a bedroom to myself." An important factor because it secured to her the possibility of a shut door, behind which the experience might take place of which Jesus spake when He said : " Shut thy door . . . and thy Father which seeth in secret Himself shall reward thee openly."

" The days were filled up with meetings. I did not feel in touch with others in the house, and needless to say I made no effort to make friends. The hours between the meetings were spent in solitary meditation. I sat in the tent day after day and heard much of deep spiritual value, yet nothing gripped me until the last morning when Hubert Brooke spoke on Deut. xviii. 6, 7. ' And if a Levite come from any of thy gates out of all Israel, where he sojourned, and come with all the desire of his mind unto the place which the Lord shall choose ; then he shall minister in the name of the Lord his God, as all his brethren the Levites do which stand there before the Lord.'

" As he spoke on coming with all the desire of one's mind to the place which the Lord chooses, the Spirit of God convicted me of a subtle discontent which was in danger of wrecking my usefulness in the new sphere which He had chosen for me. I recognized the secret of my restlessness to be that I had not come with all the desire of my *mind* into the place which the Lord had appointed. The fundamental difference between passively acquiescing in the Will of God and deliberately choosing that Will, with all the desire of the *mind*, was made vividly plain to me."

Before she left the tent that morning, the choice was made, the cloud had lifted and her heart was full of praise. Her feet now stood upon a rock, and she knew that all grace would be supplied to enable her for the work committed to her.

It was remarkable that until this time, she had met none of her friends, but before many hours had passed a lady was shown into her room. " My dear," she said, " I have been searching for you all the week and could not find you anywhere. Why did you not leave your name and address at the Convention Lodge ? I was particularly anxious to see you because a few days ago some money, which I never expected to be repaid, was given me and a strong conviction came upon me that I was to hand it all over to you, for the expenses of your house."

So saying, she handed Miss Soltau an envelope containing a cheque for fifty pounds.

Miss Soltau's mail-bags in the next few weeks made it quite clear that enlargement of premises was necessary, but before the next quarter day No. 37 Pyrland Road was ' TO LET ' and the house was taken. The fifty pounds were spent in furnishing it in a simple way, and as soon as ever it was made habitable it was required for the young women who formed the first party arriving from Sweden. It consisted of four girls who drove up unannounced, from the docks, one early morning. Behind came two cabs laden with boxes and bulging with feather bedding.

They were unable to speak a word of English, but felt immediately at home as members of a household whose inmates were drawn from many European countries. Sometimes as many as ten languages were spoken in the house, including Russian and Finnish, and one of the interesting events of each week was the Friday prayer-meeting when each was free to pray in her native tongue.

As regards Miss Soltau's inner life, its whole aspect was transfigured. In the region of thought Satan had formerly exercised power to torment her with questionings and fears, but now she was as one released from bondage, and understood what it was to be garrisoned by the peace of God not only in heart but in mind.

III

FROM the year 1889 until 1916, when, owing to war conditions, the house automatically emptied itself of students, Miss Soltau remained in charge of the Women Candidates' Department of the China Inland Mission. During that period five hundred and forty-seven of the young women who passed through her hands went to China as members of the Mission. Apart from these a very large number were drafted into other societies. Some went to South Africa, others to India, Arabia or Egypt, and when a forward movement was made to the Tibetan border, Miss Soltau had her share in it by opening her house to the members of the party. She made it her ambition that no young woman, conscious of a missionary vocation, should be prevented from fulfilling the same by reason of any disability which friendship, financial help or suitable training could overcome.

How many times testimony has been borne by a missionary whose value has come to be recognized : " Had it not been for Miss Soltau and the help which she gave me, no Mission Board would have entertained the thought of accepting me for foreign service."

To quote one : " My mother died when I was

young and from the age of sixteen I earned my living at rough work and in a rough set. When I made application to the China Inland Mission with no clear thought in my mind excepting that I was saved and that my great desire was to take the gospel to the heathen, I was noisy, assertive and loudly dressed. I remember on arrival being shown into Miss Soltau's study. When the door opened and she entered I seemed transfixed by her beautiful presence. She welcomed me kindly, listened to my story, prayed with me and asked if I had any means of paying my board during the time I might spend in her house. My total savings amounted to four pounds ten shillings and I told her so. She laughed and said: 'You will need all that for yourself, my dear, but I will take you in for a short time and you shall help in the house for your board.' This short time extended to six months, and not until the end of that time was I allowed to see the Council. I was grievously disappointed in not being able to do so earlier, but before the end of that probation I saw the wisdom of the delay. By that time I had learned to speak and dress more quietly, and how to fit into the community life."

A veteran missionary from India writes:

"When I had to make the final decision about going abroad I was torn in two. Many were saying that I was wrong to dream of leaving home, for there was one there who wanted me and, as it seemed, needed me. His friends, leaders of the Convention movement, were utterly opposed to my leaving him. Some even told me that if I left him his death would be at my door. Because those who said these things were the very saints of the earth, their words had weight. On one side there were many voices and on the other the One compelling voice. Miss Soltau, perhaps seeing or feeling my distress, came to me that night in the little bedroom at the old Pyrland Road house. The window had been open and the white dressing table cover was powdered with smuts. We stood beside it, and as a tortured heart does always notice trifles, so I noticed those smuts. The words broke from me : ' They say that if I leave him he will die— even so am I right to go ? ' She did not answer for a moment, then said solemnly, ' Yes, I think even so, that you are right to go.'

" It was a tremendous answer. She must have added something about trusting our Father to deal tenderly with His servant who had truly given me to Him, though his heart still clung to me. But all I remember of the next few minutes is, that with her arms around me I entered into peace. Often, through the many years that have passed since that night, I have been helped by the memory of her courage in the ways of God, to strengthen a younger soul who was being torn as I was then."

Another writes : " When I left College I was agnostic, pessimist and communist. I dragged my morbid moods through the gaieties of the world without securing any alleviation of my inward gloom. Shortly after my conversion I became impressed with the sense of a call to China and sent in my application to the China Inland Mission. Miss Soltau must have seen at once what an unlikely subject I was to be favourably considered by the Council. Nevertheless I received nothing but encouragement from her, and she so helped me to steer my course that I was accepted for training and two years later sailed for China. I had never read the Pilgrim's Progress, nor did I do so until I studied it in Chinese, but as soon as I read of Christian's experiences in the House of the Interpreter, I said to myself : ' This is what Miss Soltau's house was to me.' "

From North China comes the following :

" When I was home on furlough after being a prisoner in the hands of the Boxers I was constantly pressed to relate the experiences of those awful days and every time I did so I suffered agonies from nightmare. I used to fancy that thousands of men swarmed over me and that I was trying in vain to kill one of them. I told Miss Soltau of this and she, like others, had expressed sympathy, but one night in Hastings, when I had to share a room with her, she saw for herself my terrors. At the meeting I had been asked, as usual, for details and after giving them I awoke at midnight to find myself fighting Miss Soltau. Then she saw for herself what my condition was and said, 'If this goes on you will never be able to return to your work in China.' Up she got and prayed for me that I might be released from this torment and from the onslaughts of the powers of darkness. I never again was victim to that awful nightmare."

On one occasion she found two Norwegian girls living in one small room and working hard for their daily bread, in the hope of learning English and eventually being able to join one of the Norwegian missions working in China., Without delay the two girls were invited to Pyrland Road where they received skilled help in the English language, and shared all advantages of training in Christian work and Bible study. They eventually sailed for China under the escort of a C.I.M. party.

Yet another writes: "Never shall I forget, years ago, when, with an aching heart and blighted life I found my way to Miss Soltau. Though I had never spoken to her before, she met me with every kindness and after a talk said gently : 'There is One Who has been watching you all the time that you have been going on with this aching heart. He knows all about your sorrow.' Then she knelt down and just told the Lord Jesus all about it. Oh, the comfort! I went away feeling that I had been with the Lord Jesus. From that day till she died, nearly thirty-eight years later, she has been my true and faithful friend who always strengthened my hands in God. She was like one sitting in the sunshine of her Saviour's love and always drawing others into its warmth and comfort."

An intimate visitor to the house gives her impressions : " I never failed to find some interesting guest at Miss Soltau's table. Once it was Dr. Baedecker who fascinated us with stories of work in the prisons of Siberia ; another time Dr. Harry Guinness, with all the latest news from the Congo. I remember meeting Dr. William Soltau from the McAll Mission in Paris and once Dr. Hudson Taylor himself, not to speak of a constant stream of missionaries from all lands. The candidates were always an impressive group, and among the foreigners were those who bore the stamp of unusual strength of character and ability. A tall, fair Scandinavian would sit side by side with a vivacious Slav, and a stern woman in continental Deaconess dress next to a Welsh country girl. Cultured and interesting women of many nationalities were there, the whole forming one of the most perfect expressions of Christian communal life, under the serene leadership of Miss Soltau herself."

A nurse tells : " When I came back on furlough in 1924 my wrist-watch was ruined by the steam of

the steriliser and was quite useless. Miss Soltau
heard of it and immediately slipped hers on to my
arm. It is one of my greatest treasures. . . ."

One who was long an inmate of the house, writes :
" Miss Soltau never lost her child heart. Things
which brought joy and gaiety to the home circle
did not seem trivial to her. No account of her
household would be complete without a record
of the Christmas festivities she arranged for the
continental students. The English girls went home
for the vacation, leaving from six to ten foreigners
in the house. First the big class-rooms were closed
—' to save work ! ' Then there was regular way-
laying of the postman and abstraction of various
parcels from abroad. On the day previous to
Christmas Eve a big Christmas Tree was smuggled
in and safely planted in the locked class-room.
Long after the household had gone to bed Miss
Soltau and her staff spent hours in dressing it.
Those dear foreigners knew nothing of all this
and sadly bewailed our cold English customs. We
wickedly met their woe by ' thinking it so strange
for grown-ups to want a tree—children of course
did. . . .'

" At tea-time on Christmas Eve Miss Soltau
' thought it would be nice to gather for a little
time in the drawing-room,' and when she was
assured that all the family had arrived, would again
innocently suggest that the room was rather cold

or small, should they go to the class-room? Leading the way she threw open the door and to their astonished eyes, in the room lighted only by the bright fire-light and the dozens of tiny candles on its branches, stood their beloved Christmas tree!

" I can still recall the sight of literal tears of joy that ran down their cheeks when we all held hands and moving slowly round the tree joined as well as we could, in carols sung in all their different languages. After this Miss Soltau voiced the thought of all hearts as she so naturally thanked God for all this joy.

" Then the fun began. Long expected and delayed parcels suddenly appeared and for each member of the family Miss Soltau provided a real love gift

" The same tree afterwards did duty at a children's party in the Mission House, and ended its career at a Children's Treat in the slums of North London."

One of the early candidates for China went about her work carrying a secret burden of sorrow. She had a prodigal brother and felt that she could not leave the country without seeing him. At last she could bear it no longer alone and went to Miss Soltau with her story.

" We must get him to come here, my dear," said Miss Soltau.

"I do not know where he is," was Mary's answer. "Father forgave him so many times, but at last he forbade him the house and we have quite lost sight of him."

"My dear, with God nothing is impossible."

The students were taken into confidence and there was much prayer for the prodigal, but meanwhile Miss Soltau communicated with the Salvation Army and sent them a notice to be posted in each of their slum depôts.

Every arrangement was made for the brother's reception. He was to be taken straight to the drawing-room, his sister to be summoned and strong coffee was to be immediately brewed in the kitchen. All happened according to programme. One evening when the students were sitting with Miss Soltau round the fire, a somewhat shuffling step was heard coming from the gate to the front door and a knock followed.

"There he is! You go and open the door, Mary," said Miss Soltau.

They all listened and heard the visitor slowly walking up the stairs to the drawing-room.

"It must be he," said the excited students.

Meanwhile Miss Soltau went out to the kitchen and waited to take up the coffee herself, praying, as she walked upstairs, that the Lord would give her a promise from His Word, to take hold of by faith. As she went the word was given and it was this : " Shall the prey be taken from the mighty, or the lawful captive delivered ? But thus saith the Lord, Even the captives of the mighty shall be taken away and the prey of the terrible shall be delivered, for I will contend with him that contendeth with thee."

She entered the room with a smiling welcome to the visitor, who looked considerably ' down and out.'

" I cannot tell you how glad we are to see you here," she said.

She then poured out coffee, and while he was drinking it, sat down by him and said :

" I am going to tell you how you can be completely delivered from the power of drink."

" Impossible," said the poor man, mournfully shaking his head. " Impossible."

" No," she said, " it is not impossible. With God nothing is impossible." Then she told him of the Saviour's power to deliver the captive. When he seemed ready for it, she suggested prayer and the three knelt. Mary tried to pray but broke down ; Miss Soltau prayed and presently the man was heard to say, " God be merciful to me, a sinner."

Immediately Miss Soltau took up the penitent's prayer and praised the Lord for saving him. When they rose from their knees he was a new creature in Christ Jesus.

When Mary sailed for China, two months later, her brother was on the quay to see her off, a decent, self-respecting figure. He did not live long after this, and his sister rejoiced that he was safely at Home in the Father's House.

IV

SEEING that Miss Soltau now accepted no financial support from the China Inland Mission she was at complete liberty to arrange her own time and the details of her establishment as seemed best to herself. To her the *raison d'être* of a Christian community was that "rivers of living water" might flow out from it to the needy places of the earth. Some of these needy places were at her very door.

Her contact with the young women of her own neighbourhood was through the Y.W.C.A. of which she early became Local Secretary. In this connection she gave Sunday afternoon and Wednesday evening to a girls' Bible Class, and Sunday evening to an Evangelistic Service. Some of the first members were business girls whom she had met in the Holiday Home at Hastings.

Thursday evening was devoted to a Bible Class which was largely attended by Christian workers. Friday was prayer meeting night; "these were times of real intercession, for Miss Soltau's realistic way of presenting the life of the Mission Field, enabled the students to grasp the situation and encouraged them to pray pointedly concerning the needs."

The application of a good percentage of the candidates for Missionary Service was refused on account of health or for family reasons. Miss Soltau felt that if this were the end of their service for the Mission Field something was seriously wrong; so she gave much thought and prayer as to how best she might link them on to the work, that their missionary zeal should not be wasted. Thus was formed the Helping Hands Association, through whose agency an amazing number of beautifully made garments were forwarded to missionaries on the field, and a considerable sum of money was contributed.

Miss Soltau was in constant requisition as speaker at meetings and missions for young women. Her connection with the Y.W.C.A. at Richmond, Surrey, linked her with another great spiritual movement. In fact, hers was the voice which brought to its Secretary, Jessie Penn Lewis, a vision of the possibilities of the life of faith which she afterwards explored to such great purpose. Each Good Friday was a day of retreat at Pyrland Road, when several hundred people met for fellowship. These meetings were led by Jessie Penn Lewis, whose ardent enthusiasm inspired all to greater zeal.

One who helped her with the voluminous correspondence which was inevitably her daily portion, records : " She wrote many letters with her own hand and dictated many more, in addition to the heavy business arising from her position as Secretary of the Ladies' Council. Her continuity of thought and aptitude for picking up the thread if she were interrupted in the dictation of a letter, were really wonderful. I have known her come back after being called away perhaps for half an hour or longer, and resume in the middle of a sentence, as if nothing had intervened.

"Her China family will ever remember her circular letters, with the notes she took of various addresses or gathered from any source that she thought would prove helpful. It always seemed a pity that the typewriter could not reproduce the expression of her voice and face as she entered into the subject she was dictating as vividly as though her readers were before her.

"Another of her great joys was the sending of her New Year cards to all who had passed through the Training Home, and to others also. Her study in October and November might have been a small shop, and the choice of a card or calendar for each individual, was part of her joy. 'So-and-so would *love* that.'

"Her holidays were practically nil and on one occasion, when I returned from mine, she told me she had written over 300 letters with her own hand during the few days she had been away and since returning to London."

The rule of the house was 'Trust and Give.'
There was no luxury but no stint. Her table was
abundantly supplied with good food, well served.

"Living at some distance from London I used
to visit her only about once a year. Each time I
was impressed with the liberality of her hospitality.
On the occasion of a Mildmay Conference, I would
see her move among a crowd of friends who had
gathered from many quarters and ask them to lunch
at her house with the easy grace of a *châtelaine* who
knew that she could never go beyond the resources
of her home provision. Dozens of people would
walk in and partake of a delicious lunch of cold
meat, fresh salad, good bread-and-butter and a
variety of puddings. Knowing that she looked to
God for each shilling of her expenditure I received
a most gracious impression that she felt herself the
child of a very wealthy Father Who had no call to
keep her on insufficient supplies."

Only those who were admitted to the intimacies
of her private life knew how scrupulous she was
in the use of every farthing that came to her.
Nothing was wasted and nothing was grudged.
All was a sacred trust, and as was to be expected
the atmosphere of the house powerfully influenced
the students who lived in it. Many, of course,
paid their own board, but none were ever refused
because they were unable to do so. The daily
round was a perpetual reminder of Divine control

of human affairs. It was startling when the answer
to the request for a new scrubbing brush was
playfully given : " Well, dear, you must ask the
Lord to send us one, as I have nothing in my
purse." It was even more amazing to the un-
initiated to find the answer on the doorstep at
10 a.m. in the shape of the ironmonger's boy with
two scrubbing brushes tied to a carpet brush, all
addressed to Miss Soltau, and to find that neither
she nor anyone in the house had any idea where
they came from. In this particular case it was
several months before the mystery was solved, and
then only through a chance encounter. Miss Soltau
met a lady at the entrance of the ironmonger's
shop, who addressed her, saying :

" By the way, Miss Soltau, I hope you got a
broom and two brushes some months ago. I was
buying some for myself and remembering your
large family, thought you would be sure to need
some too, so I ordered them to be sent up."

On another occasion the student on kitchen
duty, still a stranger to any abnormal method of
obtaining household supplies, burst in on Miss
Soltau with the information :

" I forgot to say that we are out of coals. Can I
tell the greengrocer's boy to bring along a sack
with the greens ? "

The situation was critical. There were thirty
candidates in the house, and Miss Soltau was again

down to her last shilling. In order to gain time she said :

" Wait a little, Ellen, I must think about it."

The cause of her hesitation was that she made it a principle never to order anything unless the money to pay for it was in hand. Her manner of life made her most careful in outlay and she would not incur the smallest debt. Only one hour remained before she was due to lead the morning Bible study, and that hour was spent in communion with her Heavenly Father. So preoccupied was her mind with the business of the moment that when the bell rang to summon the household for their class she rose from her knees unable even to remember upon what subject she had intended to speak. In a moment of earnest prayer she asked that a message be given her for the waiting class, and received a conviction that she should speak upon the second chapter of the Acts of the Apostles. On her way downstairs she told Ellen to order one sack of coal, for she had been assured that the money to pay for it would be there when the time came.

Wishing to confirm her own guidance she asked the students : " Have any of you any particular subject which you would like us to consider to-gether to-day ? " Instantly a recently arrived Norwegian girl said :

" Oh, Miss Soltau, I wish you would take the second chapter of Acts with us. Having ' all things

in common,' seems to me such an unpractical way
of living."

Miss Soltau adds: "I smiled to myself as I
remembered a large cheque which I had lately
cashed for her and thought how practical some
application of it would be to my coal bill."

At this moment a visitor slipped into the back
of the room. As the Bible Class was in progress
she quietly took a seat and Miss Soltau was not
even aware of her presence.

It was no ordinary Bible reading that morning,
and far outran its limit of time before the matter
of the practicability of having 'all things in common' had been sufficiently discussed. As the
students finally rose from their knees Miss Soltau
turned and sighted her visitor.

"You little know what this hour has meant to
me," was the lady's first remark. "I now see clearly
that to which I have been feeling my way for many
months. This morning's subject makes the reason
of my visit quite easy to tell. I awoke last night
hearing distinctly the words, 'Take one pound
and give it to Miss Soltau.' I thought it was a dream
and slept again but three times the same message
came. At last I said, 'Lord, I am a poor widow,
I have only two pounds in hand and Miss Soltau
is a well-off lady.' I have often seen you in your
nice house at Hastings with the missionaries'
children whom you were supporting. How could

I offer you one pound ? At breakfast this morning I told my strange experience to my friend, and she reminded me that I needed every penny of the only two pounds I had. However, I could get no rest of mind until I started here to bring you this sovereign."

As she spoke Miss Soltau heard the rattle of the coal being shot into the cellar, and with unspeakable relief related to her visitor her own side of the story, ending by showing her the purse with its content of one shilling.

Miss Soltau's testimony is as follows : " For fourteen months on end I never had enough on Monday to carry us through the week, yet never once were the tradesmen's books left unpaid on Saturday. Many times the laundry money, to a penny, came on Monday morning, and sometimes when I had to take a short journey by train some thankoffering was given me which exactly covered my fare. The needs were so much larger than those of the Hastings house, but the supplies were ever according to the requirement and gradually all fear vanished from my heart, as I was taught that my Lord held the supplies."

About this time one of the intimate circulars which she addressed to China friends told them of a present received which, personally, gave her the greatest joy. " You know that my dream has long been to have a little Mission Hall of our own on the piece of spare land near the C.I.M. house. Now what do you think our Father has done ? Given me a little hall, to seat 150, with all gas-fittings, stove, harmonium, cupboard full of china (for teas) and 100 chairs in it ! I must tell my story in few words : The hall is at Bromley, Kent, on Lord Kinnaird's grounds. He sold the estate and the hall must be moved, so he offered it to my brother-in-law, Mr. Hill, who did not want it, but my sister instantly thought of our need, so he wrote off to Lord Kinnaird and asked him to give it to me instead ! The letter did not reach him for ten days and meantime two other applications came. We were praying and praising, too, for we thought it all so wonderful, that it must be the Lord's provision. Lord Kinnaird's answer came at last : ' Given with much pleasure.' After weighing the matter he decided that we should make the most use of it ! We sang the Doxology over and over again round the breakfast table."

V

IN 1896 Dr. and Mrs. Hudson Taylor were home in England and it was brought to their notice that it would be well, from many points of view, for Miss Soltau to take a holiday and visit China.

The suggestion was not quite so limpid as it sounded, and Miss Soltau strongly resented what she viewed as interference with her private affairs. Some considered that there was danger of the Women's Department becoming so centred in Henrietta Soltau, that no one else would ever be able to handle it. Some also suggested that it would be gain both to Miss Soltau and to certain individuals, who made exorbitant claims on her time and strength, if something could intervene to cut the connection.

It was Miss Soltau's life dream to visit the country to whose interests she had devoted all her energies, but both the manner and the moment of the suggestion roused her antagonism.

Her sister-in-law Mrs. George Soltau was on her way home from Australia and was free and willing to take Henrietta's place as head of the home. Dr. and Mrs. Hudson Taylor were returning to China, *via* America, with Miss Bessie Hanbury

who would care for her on the journey, and every
objection she made was countered by the evidence
of some suitable provision for the need.

Finally, on November 28, 1897, the party left
Euston for Liverpool to sail by the s.s. *Germanic*
for New York. One who was present writes :
" The pain of that departure will not be forgotten
by those who witnessed it. Henrietta tried to keep
up appearances, but there was no hiding her distress.
N. was there, weeping stormily, and quite thought-
less of all the suffering she was bringing on
Henrietta."

It was truly an unpropitious beginning for a
visit which should have been a great joy to her and
to her large family in China. She was learning a
lesson in the school for foreign missionaries which
was going to enlarge her understanding of the
peculiar sorrows of that strangely tried body. It
took a while for the bleeding roots to heal, and
there was no gaiety as she launched forth.

The travellers' daily programme was organized
on the conventional lines then regarded as *de
rigueur* for a party of missionaries on board ship.
It is in some cases easier to read the truth between
the lines of the journal kept at this time, than to
arrive at it from the actual words she wrote. She
speaks of " blessing and help received from the
daily Bible Readings conducted by dear Dr. Taylor
which I never feel I can miss," on the other hand she

refers to the " misery of struggling to these meetings
with a swimming head and suffering all the wretchedness of sea-sickness."

It is easy to see with what relief she subsided
into a state of passive contemplation as soon as
the exacting morning meeting was concluded,
though she had to pull herself together once more
in time to join the party at evening prayers. She
remarks with some wonder on " Dr. Taylor's
evident enjoyment of an ocean voyage," but from
this hour her sympathy was given with more
understanding to any young missionary of whom
it might be reported with some measure of censure,
that she was slack in attending the daily meetings
for Bible reading and prayer, or that on several
occasions she had absented herself from these
gatherings.

As the days went by she felt better, and had
the experience of intercourse with all and sundry
of her fellow-passengers. " My vocation at present
seems to be entirely with young men who seek
me out and tell me their stories." When the
party reached New York, the misery of sea-
sickness gave place to the suffering of home-
sickness. She remembered the familiar circle at
Pyrland Road and longed intensely to share its
activities again. The speed of life in the States
bewildered her, and the long train journeys involv-
ing the unaccustomed use of sleepers, luxurious

dining-cars and an unfamiliar organization of her days, seemed to accentuate her longing for the intensive life to which she was accustomed.

Dr. and Mrs. Taylor were carried off to be the guests of Dr. Pierson, while Miss Soltau and Miss Hanbury were conducted to apartments at the Central Y.W.C.A. " We made ourselves known to the ladies in the office, who supplied us with an elaborate paper to be filled in before they would entrust us with the keys of our heated rooms. Having given in detail our names, ages, denominations, and references, together with domicile and destination, we were glad to make our way to a restaurant where we could secure a cup of tea."

From New York she was whirled to Toronto and thence to Chicago as guest of the Moody Bible Institute. Here she was genuinely impressed, both with the style of the students and their number. Most of all she marvelled at the amount of independence given to them. " They are all so very free," she wrote home, " but one feels this in the States. At home we are much more reserved. They received us genially and cordially, in Christ's Name, and then used us so constantly that every hour seemed to be bought up. May God bless these dear friends and repay them for all their love to us."

On the Sunday afternoon she attended Dr. Torrey's Bible Class for adults, having a desire herself to learn something of the plan of conducting meetings of this character on so large a scale. Before the close Dr. Torrey espied her, and speaking from the platform said : " I have just discovered that Miss Henrietta Soltau is among us. She is the daughter of Henry Soltau to whom we owe so much for his writings, and who is now in glory. I will ask her to speak a few words before we separate."

Mounting the platform Miss Soltau gave a brief address, at the close of which Dr. Torrey appealed to the unconverted members of the audience to make a decision for Christ. In a few moments many were rising to their feet in distant parts of the hall, and at once Miss Soltau felt herself back in the thrilling atmosphere of the great Moody Mission meetings. A tall Norwegian in the front row was sobbing, and Miss Soltau sat down beside him and led him to the Saviour. Some enthusiastic negresses hailed her to " give a word about the Master."

" I get my doubts and fears, sister," said one.

" Aye," replied the other, " we don't praise enough. It's praising keeps the devil at bay."

A few days later they were at San Francisco, where they joined the s.s. *City of Peking*, reaching Honolulu on Christmas Day in time to spend some hours with kind and hospitable friends, and for the first time Miss Soltau had the pleasure of seeing a crowd of one thousand Chinese seated in a Church.

The thrill came when the steamer slowly entered the mouth of the river at Woosung outside Shanghai, and all around her were the people for whom she had lived, prayed and toiled for years. The travellers made ready to land, but before they touched the wharf their deck was swarming with chattering coolies. In the midst was a calm, quiet, competent Britisher whose word every coolie seemed to obey. He was the missionary in charge of Transport for the C.I.M., one of the fine group who serve their Lord in serving their fellow workers.

All baggage was left to him, the party safely put into rickshaws, and at full speed the coolies ran them through the crowded, narrow streets towards the Headquarters of the C.I.M. in Woosung Road.

VI

SHE alighted from her rickshaw and stepped from the noisy thoroughfare into a quiet compound. The wide enclosure was surrounded on three sides by low buildings whose rooms opened on shady verandahs. Looking around her she could scarcely credit that it was she, Henrietta Soltau, who stood there.

Everyone was out to greet the party, and she received the first of all the missionary welcomes that were to be hers. Outwardly she was all warm response, but inwardly she was prey to a strange mood, and the piles of letters waiting on her bedroom table brought her less joy than torment.

There were letters from 41A Pyrland Road, telling of alterations in the routine, suggesting comparisons and making small criticisms. She saw the likelihood of all that had been so vital to her, in the financial support of the house, becoming common talk and losing the sacredness of its intimate character.

There were letters regarding students, Bible Class members and candidates, which made her shrink, for in them was recorded in plain language, faults and failings of which she had always been aware, but which, looked at with the eye of love, had not appeared so repellent as they now did under the scrutiny of a calm, cool, critical eye. That hurt. Lastly there was a pile of epistles from a few who showered a selfish, exacting love upon her. Henrietta Soltau was an easy victim to such. She fascinated them and was unable to protect herself from their perpetual demands, seeing that they were always clamorous in the region of the soul.

She came down the stairs at the sound of the dinner bell, dreading the crowds, the talk, the questions and the strangeness of it all.

The long dining tables were crowded with missionaries and their families, for it was Christmas holidays and the scholars of the Chefoo Schools were spending the vacation with their parents who had travelled from the interior to meet them at Shanghai.

Chinese table boys moved swiftly about the room with artistic economy of movement, carrying large dishes of vegetables and rice, their vigilant eyes noting any who were not supplied.

In the buzz of general talk she sat rather silent, grappling with the problem which was to embitter those early China days, namely the sense of having somehow missed the will of God and been led off into doing things which were not part of His plan. It seemed impossible for her to throw off the feeling that she had not received her command to visit China direct from God, as was her wont, but had been coerced by the will of man. She had no liberty in her spirit. During those difficult Shanghai days, although her outward serenity seemed unruffled, her inner being was a prey to doubts, as is shown by her correspondence with one intimate friend. It was well for Henrietta Soltau that the woman who received her confidences knew both how to keep her secret and how to speak faithfully and fearlessly to one older than herself when she saw her in danger of wrecking the value of a unique opportunity.

"Beloved friend," she wrote, "each of your letters deepens my conviction that the adversary is gaining a subtle advantage over you which may frustrate the value of the opportunity which is now yours. You have been given a privilege that, some day, you will marvel at. . . .

"When you emerge you will find that you cannot doubt His hand in leading you forth to China. . . . It would have been so easy for God to stop you. . . . Is it likely that He would have let you make such a serious mistake as to go to China against His will? I cannot believe it. . . . The enemy has found out the spot at which to aim his dart: 'your fault,' 'you missed the will of God,' 'you should have waited.' . . . That you have no power to lay the anguish down, shows how it has

gripped you. . . . The devil has haunted you
with the horror of a mistaken step. . . .

" It is well that your old household should be
cut off from you. . . . You were too much to
them. . . . Do not try to hold on to the English
claims. . . . As to finance at Pyrland Road, let
God manage His own affairs. . . .

" It is never the will of God that responsibility
for souls you cannot reach, should hinder responsibility for what is at your hand. . . . The power
of darkness has contrived this in England to
paralyze you in China. . . .

" Come, leave God's souls to God. . . . He
has others to do the work at Mildmay, do you enter
into His world-wide purposes. Let go all thought
of when and how He will send you back. You must
be free as the wind to be moved as He listeth. . . .
We cannot be fully in the waters to swim in, so
long as we think of the bank."

Later the tone of the letters changes and her
friend writes : " Thank God that at last you are
in Himself again—a great calm—A.B. is safe under
His watching. Let go. He had to take you to China
for this."

It would appear that Henrietta Soltau, so valiant
in the region of faith, failed on this one point as
other saints have done—she could trust God to
forgive her sins, to heal her body, to supply her
needs, but could not believe that He would keep

her, His willing, obedient child, from making mistakes in His service. Under her friend's reproof she saw her failing and sought grace to free herself from the disturbing influences of Pyrland Road and to live a unified and abundant life in the place where she was.

VII

BEFORE starting inland Miss Soltau was taken about to visit Shanghai and was shown the activities of the various missionary societies at work in that place. Everything interested her, and the accounts of rescue work among the child-prostitutes of the port moved her so deeply that she willingly accepted an invitation to visit the houses in which the wretched little victims carried on their trade.

"Come and see for yourself, it is better than taking any second-hand report," said the one who offered to be her guide.

To her surprise the houses were palaces, not dens, located in the British Concession, and built or rented by Westerners. "Room after room was filled with opium-smokers, each two lying opposite the other, with their lamps and pipes between them, their heads resting on wooden pillows. Many of the men were handsomely dressed in gay silks, some sleeping heavily, others only half stupefied. Here and there at square tables, painted and gorgeously dressed girls were seated, drinking tea. Some of them were only ten to twelve years of age. We wandered on over three floors. Into this one building alone, some four thousand people press every night. As we left the place a fight was in progress—shouting, pushing, gesticulating—a rowdy crowd through which we had to force our way to gain the street. I am told that there are one thousand one hundred such opium palaces in the Foreign Concessions, to say nothing of innumerable dens in the Chinese quarter.

Dr. Hudson Taylor decided that no time should be lost in securing the end for which Miss Soltau had come to China, which was to see inland stations and the conditions of missionary life there. It was accordingly arranged that on February 14th she should leave for Chinkiang, travel up to the Women's Training Home at Yangchow and thence to other stations on the Grand Canal.

It is from one's personal knowledge of the discomforts of journeys by houseboat in wintry weather that one realizes all that Miss Soltau was called upon to endure. Her journals scarcely hint at the difficulties, and her fine capacity for making the best of things stood her in good stead.

If she was silent about the wretchedness of damp and cold at Yangchow, she was equally uncomplaining of the June heat and mosquitoes at the Men's Training Home, Anking.

One who was a student at the time records: " There was an unusually large number of men recruits in the Language School at Anking in the winter 1897–98 and a very happy spirit prevailed, as is usually the case. But there was a hunger in the hearts of many for a deeper knowledge of God and this found expression in the gathering together of small groups of three or four in the Students' Rooms for prayer that God would do ' a new thing ' for us all, so that, ere we left the Language School, we might be more fully equipped spiritually, for the conflict in which we were to be engaged.

" None of us thought at that time that four of our number were to have the honour of joining ' the noble army of martyrs,' and that all of us would have to pass through the strain and anguish which will for ever be associated in the minds of China missionaries with the ' Boxer ' year (1900). God knew what was before us and how we needed to know Him more fully if we were to be ready for the new experiences, and He had His plan for meeting the need.

" As the days went on the study of the Chinese language became more and more absorbing and a healthy rivalry sprang up in the desire to pass our first examination while still at the Language School.

" One morning the Principal told us that Miss Soltau was coming on a visit and hoped to hold a few meetings with us. We were all very loath to allow anything to break into our study and a feeling almost akin to resentment was stirred within us.

" A few of us went as a deputation to the Principal to suggest that, in view of the near approach of our examination, Miss Soltau should be asked just to speak at our usual Family Prayers, possibly extending the time for a few minutes. To this he wisely agreed and on her arrival Miss Soltau cordially fell in with the arrangement. This was carried out on the first morning after her arrival, but so great was the power of the brief message that the same deputation went to the Principal again and asked that next day the time should be extended.

" Before many days were over the whole morning and the evening were spent in listening to Miss Soltau's messages and in prayer as, out of her rich spiritual experiences, she gave us of her best.

" What a time it was for us all! New vision of the power of prayer came to us as she told us some of those wonderful stories of her own life. There was new wonder in the Word as it was opened to us day by day, and a new sense of the need of the Chinese around us who were without Christ.

" It verily was a gracious revival from the presence of the Lord and made all the difference to the life and ministry of more than thirty missionaries.

" Rivers of living water truly flowed through the Lord's servant and they touched the very ends of China."

Before leaving Anking she composedly records:
" A riot threatened us here some days ago. The
missionaries wished to avail themselves of the
presence of the many students taking their examin-
ations, to make a free distribution of books as they
left the Halls. Nearly all the students had accepted
these very graciously, when a number of roughs
began forcibly to snatch the books from them and
lighted a bonfire. Fighting ensued and the missionaries might have suffered much harm but for the
refuge offered by a guard-house conveniently near,
until such time as, under military guard, they were
escorted home. The Official wired to the Consul
to urge us to act in accordance with the words in
Matthew vii. 6, ' Give not that which is holy unto
the dogs, neither cast ye your pearls before swine,
lest they trample them under their feet and turn
and rend you.' " The scriptural knowledge of the
Official is striking as compared with his ignorance
of meteorological phenomena, for Miss Soltau
continues : " He closed the North Gate hoping
to bring fine weather, and ordered the soldiers to
curse heaven and fire several volleys in order to
disperse the showers."

After visiting Anking and Yangchow she wrote
as follows : " Uphold these young people day by
day in prayer. What will be their fight of faith ?
Will their race be long or short ? Will they endure
to the end ? There is nothing easy in life in China.

Here they meet the powers of darkness unveiled, one feels them in the very air, and in the awful sounds that greet the ear one hears the power of the adversary. The eyes see sights that one cannot record on paper—iniquity, evil, filthiness everywhere. Get to your knees and fight the battle with these young workers. Here there is no safety except as we abide under the shadow of the Almighty. I realize more than ever that I could never say to anyone, ' Come to China,' the responsibility would be too great."

July found her at Chefoo visiting the large C.I.M. Schools for missionaries' children, fruition of her own early work. In this healthy seaside place, beside Boys', Girls', and Preparatory Schools, was a Sanatorium and Hospital for the use of the missionaries. August was spent at Kuling, a hill resort in Central China where a large number of missionaries of many societies met together in Conference. In view of subsequent events, and the persecution which broke out in 1900, her report of this Conference is significant.

Writing on August 20, 1898, she says : " I was impressed with the keynote running through every testimony, the expression of readiness to lay down life for Christ's sake. The possibility of a martyr's death is before some who have been getting heavenly visions during these quiet days and coming to understand more deeply the way of following the Lamb. At the closing meeting many rose and testified to their deeper surrender of all to Him they love. More than two hundred of us gathered round the Lord's Table at a most solemn Communion Service, conducted by three Presbyterian missionaries. All differences were submerged and the presence of the Master was the one theme."

The autumn months were spent in visiting Mission stations in the provinces of Chekiang and Kiangsi. Everywhere she was welcomed by old students. In the development of some she had cause to rejoice. The lack of advance in others, she deplored.

She easily adapted herself to every household she visited—ate Chinese food, wore Chinese dress and travelled in a wheelbarrow, taking her Chinese bedding everywhere with her.

In one house two strong-minded occupants lived very simply and, as nearly as possible, like native women. Miss Soltau apparently never observed that they were skirtless like the women around them, and had not even donned, as she might have expected, the ceremonial skirt to welcome her. Next morning, however, not only they but she also appeared at breakfast in trousers. Nor did she wear her skirt again until she left that station.

The first of January, 1899, found her once more at Yangchow, on the 5th February she reached

Shanghai, and on the 25th February boarded the s.s. *Sachsen* for London via Suez.

Miss Soltau had travelled for thirteen consecutive months during which she covered six thousand miles. She had visited forty-four Mission Stations, living with the missionaries in their own homes, and she came away a wiser woman. The impressions she received largely altered the view-point from which she considered her own work in London. She now understood, as never before, what constituted the peculiar difficulties of the mission field. This phrase ceased to convey to her mind a vague impression of nebulous problems and hereafter bristled with concrete examples of incidents which she herself had witnessed. The arrival of a new worker at an inland station! What tremendous issues might be involved. She had now seen the harmony of a formerly happy household shattered by the addition to it of a young woman whose temperamental peculiarities she had noted during training days, but failed to recognize as of sufficient importance to warrant her application being refused.

Wider experience now showed her how the rigid or domineering attitude of a Senior might wreck the career of her Junior. She had heard of the tragedy of unsuitable marriages on the field, but now realized the stark pathos of a man, or woman, warped by the partnership of an ill-considered alliance. On the other hand it had become clear that two congenial fellow-workers could accomplish amazing things when their comradeship was such that time and strength were neither wasted in exacting demands nor dissipated by friction. From that time on she rejoiced exceedingly in the stable friendships which no circumstances do more to develop than the circumscribed conditions of lonely mission stations.

The necessity for the missionary of ability to stand alone, to think independently, to be free from jealousy, and to work harmoniously with those who, though their method of expression might differ, were one in their objective, became more evident to her. Above all she realized profoundly that spiritual inspiration must be gained through direct communion with God, so that in places and on occasions where sympathy fails and where fellowship is denied, the missionary will still remain unmoved and unafraid. These were among the many reflections which occupied her mind during the long sea-voyage.

Leaving the boat at Genoa, she purposed to travel home by way of Paris, that she might visit her brother William at the McAll Mission and so avoid the dreaded billows of the Bay of Biscay.

She arrived in Paris on March 30th and spent a happy Easter there, but a few days later an urgent telegram from Russia arrived, pressing her to proceed at once to St. Petersburg where Mrs. Penn Lewis was lying dangerously ill. Mrs. Penn Lewis had gone to Russia at the insistence of a Christian circle whose members were desirous to share in the revelation of Christian truth which she had been imparting to companies of believers in many countries of Europe. While there she became very seriously ill, so much so that her life hung in the balance and her friends were praying day and night, pleading with God that she might be healed.

In every emergency Mrs. Penn Lewis was in the habit of turning to Miss Soltau as to a woman who knew her God and could do exploits. In this extremity all she could advise her Russian friends was to send for Miss Soltau ; and this they did.

The summons was insistent, and Miss Soltau left Paris immediately for St. Petersburg, where she arrived on April 14th to find her friend even more dangerously ill than she had anticipated. Shortly after the patient was given assurance of recovery, and from that hour her condition improved and she began to regain strength.

Meanwhile Miss Soltau was in demand for Bible Readings and meetings among the secret disciples, who met in the upper room of a palace. This room was large enough to hold an audience of a hundred people, but was so constructed that its entrance could not be found except by the initiated. While the meetings were in progress the Princess had her own trusted watchmen out in the street, in the corridors and on the staircases leading up to the turret, who were instructed to indicate by signs if any attempt were made to take the congregation by surprise.

In silence the congregation gathered, hungry for the Word of God. Some were peasants who came with baskets of vegetables on their arms, as though they had been selling at the kitchen door. In order to attract less attention every entrance to the palace was used. Some came by the stable yard, others by the kitchen door and a few only drove up to the main entrance.

In the upper room they sat, a silent, eager concourse, desiring to be fed with the Bread of Life. This Miss Soltau broke and dispensed to them. The singing of hymns was impossible, but with hearts aglow they heard of that other upper room where, in a season of danger and bewilderment, Christ Himself stood in the midst and breathing on His disciples said : " Receive ye the Holy Ghost."

Princess and peasant knew no difference of rank as they met with their Lord in the ecstasy of His realized presence and found there the Divine solution of all social problems. As in the Early Church, the rule of Christ was recognized and it was realized that he was greatest who loved and served the best.

Of these Russian friends Miss Soltau wrote some years later : " As far as I know all these good women are with the Lord. The beloved Princess and her sister were imprisoned in their country house where they were almost starved to death, and compelled to endure the rigours of the terrible Russian winter, without fires. One died in a workman's cottage, in greatest poverty ; some were slain by the maddened crowd, yet all were full of joy in the assurance of the prize which no man could snatch from them."

Within a few days Mrs. Penn Lewis was pronounced out of danger, and Miss Soltau prepared to leave for England. Before she did so, however, a telegram came announcing the death of her beloved sister Agnes Hill. It seemed to her that there was nothing which could have so completely robbed her home-coming of joy, and with an aching heart she boarded the train for her long journey.

The entry in her diary on Monday, April 24, reads : " Home once more. His mercy endureth for ever."

VIII

NEWS of the Boxer massacres in China during the year 1900 burst on the western world with devastating suddenness. The era of prosperity which marked the close of the nineteenth century throughout the British Empire exercised a soporific effect on the minds of men, inducing a materialistic philosophy prepared to believe that the Golden Age had been ushered in which must secure ever-increasing peace and progress, in every realm of life, to a people so evidently enjoying the special favour of God. Christian martyrdom, on any large scale, seemed to the churches a contingency as remote as did a world-wide war, yet both were imminent.

On November 4th, 1898, during Miss Soltau's stay in Shanghai, news had come of the murder of Mr. Fleming, and a Miao evangelist. Commenting on the event in a letter to a friend she wrote : " I shall never forget Dr. Hudson Taylor's agony on receiving the telegram. He paced the long verandah of the Shanghai compound baffled and perplexed."

For thirty-three years men and women had traversed the Chinese Empire unprotected by any human agency. They had broken up new territory and marched forward as the vanguard of Christ's conquering army. Through all the criticism which had been levelled at the China Inland Mission, its founder and its methods of work, all had been compelled to admit that a special protection had guarded lives exposed to no ordinary measure of danger. It seemed as though an intuitive insight was now revealing to its founder the fact that the Mission must brace itself to sustain a new and terrifying method of attack. He saw that the restraining hand which had held the enemy in check was withdrawn and now the blood of the martyrs might have to flow as it had done in other ages of the world's history. Dr. Taylor wept and prayed for the safety of the lonely workers scattered over the vast continent, and awe fell on those who watched the distress of his spirit, for he evidently foresaw that this would be no isolated incident of martyrdom.

In the mercy of God, when the Boxer year came, during which more than eighty members of the C.I.M. and their children were killed, Dr. Hudson Taylor's power of perception was less acute and it was in the quiet shelter of a little Swiss town that he, in great weakness, heard the tragic news.

It was during the Keswick Convention of 1900 that there reached England the first report of martyrdom—the massacre of Emily Whitchurch and Edith Searell in the province of Shansi. This

was soon followed by further news of entire
missionary communities being wiped out. It was
a memorable Convention at which, in solemn
silence, the vast crowd was brought to a realization of what might be entailed on any individual
entering upon a pathway of obedience to Christ's
command.

As soon as the Convention closed Miss Soltau
was back in London, anxious to contribute what
help she might in breaking news to agonized
friends, and in comforting parents who were
besieging the C.I.M. Headquarters for news of
their children.

Before long distressed letters from Shanghai
were telling of the arrival of many who had
escaped from the interior. Merchants and traders,
along with missionaries, were driven from all the
inland provinces to the coast, so that Shanghai
could scarcely contain the refugees. It was obvious
that there could be no question of re-assembling
candidates for the autumn session. Indeed the
most competent authorities were of opinion that
some years must elapse before passports could be
issued.

Miss Soltau at this time writes : " I was overwhelmed as I thought of my four houses in Pyrland
Road left empty, and of the years which might
elapse before young women could again face life
in China. Alone in prayer one day it came to me

with special force what deprivations must have been suffered by those who had fled from their stations leaving everything behind. It was more than likely that many would have no suitable clothes, no provision of any kind for the cold weather and little enough money to meet their pressing needs. Many would be returning to England and would require outfits for the journey, and I prayed most earnestly that God would show me how I could help in this matter.

" On the first of September I received a cheque for twenty pounds to spend as I thought well, so I immediately used it to buy such articles as under-clothing, brushes and combs, soap, handkerchiefs, etc. Of these I made twelve parcels which I freighted to Shanghai and from that time scarcely a day passed which did not bring me money which I was free to use in this way. Sometimes it came by post, at other times it was slipped into my letter box, and I soon began to receive parcels of clothing of every description.

" I could not tell how people knew of the great need, and it seemed as if my thought had taken wings, as from Scotland and Ireland, as well as from every part of England, the supplies came pouring in. We could scarcely get boxes made, packed and freighted in time to make room for fresh supplies, and the gifts overflowed the rooms which we had cleared to receive them. We rapidly sent off fifty-two large cases besides many smaller boxes which held hats and other light articles. The clothing was of all descriptions and suitable to men, women and children. The need among the missionaries was pressing, and one fur cloak travelled back and forth to China three times.

" By late autumn large numbers of missionaries were arriving in England, many of whom had lost all their possessions. Each party was met at the docks with a letter telling its members to see me before attempting to outfit, and in every case I was able to supply all immediate necessities. Most remarkable indeed was the way in which the provision met the special need.

" I received one day a large box of men's clothing in which were three good suits, a new overcoat and a good supply of underwear. On lifting the coat I noticed the unusual length of the sleeve and it was immediately brought to my mind that Mr. A., who, with his wife, was within four days of reaching England, was a man with unusually long arms. A few days later they came in, toil-worn, weary and poorly clad. I said to Mr. A. :

" ' I will see to outfitting your wife if you will look through these clothes and see if any are suitable to you.'

" He laughingly answered : ' You cannot fit me, Miss Soltau, my arms are too long for ready-mades.'

" ' Don't be too sure,' I replied, ' my shop is different from all others, I can fit everybody.'

" A few minutes later he reappeared dressed in a good suit which might have been made for him, the length of the sleeves being exactly suitable.

" On another occasion a Swedish lady arrived, shivering with cold. How she got through the journey in winter, so thinly clothed, I did not know. I asked her to tell me what she would like best of all.

" ' Oh,' she said, ' a pair of fur-lined boots.'

" ' Here they are,' I was able to answer, ' they only came in last night.'

" The poor girl burst into tears as she tried them on and they were found to fit her exactly.

" A letter from the C.I.M. Headquarters in Shanghai told me that the house was very short of blankets for the refugees, of whom seven hundred were assembled in the compound during autumn and winter. I was able to send them out one hundred and twenty blankets at a time, all bought with the gifts of money which so continually poured in.

" A clergyman and his wife arrived one day in great need, he had lost everything, even his Bible. On this occasion, too, a box had reached me a few days ahead. It came from a clergyman's widow asking if the clothing belonging to her late husband could be of use. He had died three years previously and she had never felt that she could part with the things which he had worn until the present need had made her realize the claim of God upon them. The box she sent contained a complete clerical outfit which entirely supplied this particular missionary's need, even to a Bible, which was the facsimile of the one looted by the Boxers.

" One day I had an angry letter from the mother of a young missionary. Her daughter had lost *everything*, in her flight from the station, and was now on her way home for furlough. She said she would not replace any of the things her daughter had lost. She hated Missions. ' My daughter would have done far better to stay at home. The C.I.M. will have to look after her now.'

" I wrote back a soothing letter, and said I was sending a box over to her house to await her daughter's arrival. I kept the key myself until the daughter arrived ! When I sent it I asked Mary to let her mother see her unpack the box. Everything she could possibly need was there—two dresses, a winter coat, a full set of underlinen and even a brush and comb. There was all that she would require for many months. The mother quite broke down, astonished at the Lord's provision and her own daughter's testimony to His wonderful care over her !

" It was the abundance which was so delightful and the beautiful quality of most of the clothes supplied. Having some money in hand I thought it might be best spent on boots and shoes. Walking down Queen Victoria Street I saw a sale advertised in a large boot store Entering, I saw on the floor a heap of nice-looking leather boots. On enquiry I was told that they were reduced to half-a-crown a pair as the whole lot was made up of out sizes and under sizes. They were of excellent quality and I bought the whole heap. They proved a boon indeed to friends in Shanghai, the smaller sizes being suitable for the large numbers of children who were there with their parents.

" In all during these months three hundred pounds in gold passed through my hands besides the wealth of good clothing. Many times my cup of joy ran over, as I saw men and women who had suffered the loss of all things for Christ's sake, walk out from my house comfortably clothed, in good, well-cut garments as became those who looked for the supply of every need to the Father's hand."

The Candidates' Department was not closed down for so long a period as Miss Soltau had at first anticipated. In January, 1901, the house was re-opened to receive a party from Sweden " come to take the place of their martyred sisters." Within a few months some English candidates also applied for admission, and as early as September, 1901, the first party sailed for China.

Life in Pyrland Road resumed its normal aspect.

Strange to relate, applications were not again so numerous, nor were the parties of new workers so large or so frequent as they had previously been. Those, however, who responded to the call of Christ and gave their lives to labour in China at this time, found a door of opportunity flung wide before them and were granted a unique privilege— that of ministering to members of a Church that had experienced the ordeal of a baptism of suffering.

IX

IN 1903 Miss Soltau was able to move from Pyrland Road into two larger and more convenient houses situated in Grosvenor Road, Highbury. On June 10th she sat down for the last time in her little office from which streams of blessing had, according to her petition, flowed to the uttermost parts of the earth, and wrote as follows to a friend : " Just one line, this last day in my dear little room in 41A. It seems like a dream that we are really leaving the place so sacred with a thousand hallowed memories, linked with martyr lives and with hundreds of God's beloved scattered in many lands, and many in the Glory land.

" Now that the rooms are empty they seem shabby, and when I think of our unrighteous and miserly old landlord I am thankful that my dealings with him are over. Although the houses in Grosvenor Road are not yet ready for us we must move to-morrow, for the troublesome workmen whom he has put in have already built up the divisions between the different houses, and you can imagine the mess. . . . I am very tired, but memories crowd in upon me. Some day we shall read the story of these thirteen and a half years in the light of God's presence. To Him be all

the praise and honour and glory for ever and ever.
Amen.

"Farewell, Beloved. We are pilgrims and
strangers and this is not our rest."

On July 10th a meeting was held in the garden
of 90 Grosvenor Road to dedicate the house to
God. For a time the accommodation seemed
spacious, but within two years it proved inadequate,
and Miss Soltau was praying that the premises
might be enlarged by the addition of either 88 or
94 Grosvenor Road. "A big request," she
acknowledged, "but the need is great." Before
many months were over the landlord of 94 called
with an offer to sell the property, but there were no
funds in hand for purchase and the matter could
go no further.

Then the answer came in the person of an old
friend whose mother had recently died and who
announced that she was looking for a house where
she could live quite close to Miss Soltau and help
her "dear friend" with the work. The only snag
was that the help she desired to give was that of
taking over all the Bible study! This gave Miss
Soltau rather a fright and she writes, "Prayer was
my only resource."

The matter was settled most happily, for a short
while after a letter came which relieved Miss Soltau
of all embarrassment; it announced that the lady
was going to make someone very happy by marrying

him. However she made good her promise to help Miss Soltau and bought 94 Grosvenor Road for her, " to be a house for your old age."

Miss Soltau wrote: "In wonderful ways, through unexpected gifts, I met all expenses of the alterations needed in throwing the houses together, opening doorways on landings and also between the gardens. I asphalted the large coal-house, put in a window and turned it into a good packing-room."

The Women's Candidate Department still sustained its cosmopolitan nature, and this inevitably led to a journey on which Miss Soltau visited the various continental centres from which foreign students were drawn.

On April 10th, 1908, she left England for Germany. The first visit was to Barmen and Elberfeld where she met a circle of people who were deeply interested in missionary work, and especially in that of the China Inland Mission.

From there she went to the Bibelhaus, at Freien-walde, where she was the guest of the Baroness von Hochstetter, her two daughters and Fraulein Wasserzug.

From there she writes : " The beautiful Bibelhaus has been built with room for forty students, and there the Countess Baudissin lives with them. It is a lovely spot surrounded by the forest. Just now everything is bursting into spring bloom.

More than one hundred workers have already gone
out from the Bibelhaus all over Germany and the
Continent of Europe, and some to lonely places
on the foreign field.

"Everyone is busy preparing for the Easter
Conference. Two hundred guests have arrived to
take part in it, among whom is Sister Eva, from
Friedenshort, on the frontier of Poland, with many
of her deaconesses; ladies have come from all
parts, Denmark, Sweden, Norway, Finland and
even the borders of Russia.

"Easter Sunday dawned with beautiful sunshine
and we found the breakfast table prettily decorated
by the sisters from the Bibelhaus with sprigs of
periwinkle and other flowers, some very daintily
arranged in painted egg-shells, and the large snail
shells, while there seemed to be flowers everywhere. At the end of the table in leaves and violets,
was written 'A Blessed Easter Day.' The sisters
stood outside on the path and sang beautiful hymns
in German, then one for me in English. In the
afternoon the barn was crowded with country
people. After the ordinary service was over Pastor
Lohmann asked me to speak, which I did for over
an hour, Miss Wasserzug translating, and the
interest never flagged.

"On Tuesday we were up very early and off in
the pony carriage for the train to Berlin. It was
bitterly cold, and the journey was a slow one, but

we reached the city about ten o'clock and were soon in the Y.M.C.A. Hall where the ladies were gathering, many having spent the night in Berlin. Soon Frau von Bethmann Hollweg arrived, Miss Collet from Denmark, and quite a party with her. I was amused to find the gentlemen coming in as well as the ladies. We had a large meeting in the afternoon when I was allowed half-an-hour to speak on China.

" Wednesday, Thursday and Friday were the days of the Conference. . . . The meetings were crowded, many sitting in an ante-room where everything could be heard though nothing seen. . . . I should have liked to stay longer in beautiful Freienwalde, but I had to leave for the long journey to Liebenzell. . . .

" A large group gathered round the carriage and sang me away with hymns, and later on as the train passed near the Bibelhaus they were close to the railway line waving to me. What a gathering it will be in the Homeland when from every kindred and nation, people, and tongue we meet before His Throne to sing the praises of Him Who has redeemed us with His precious blood.

" The journey was long and I did not reach Liebenzell till half-past three. I found myself in this most lovely place in the centre of the Black Forest with all its beautiful scenery. . . . I had a very warm welcome from Pastor and Mrs. Coerper and felt it indeed a privilege to see such a centre of the Lord's work.

"Here again a whole group of students collected to say 'good-bye,' and sang me away with their lovely hymns. When I got into the train for Flushing I felt most grateful to the Lord for all the love and kindness shown to me in Germany."

The immediate result of this trip was an influx of Continental students, but its most important outcome was the effect of Miss Soltau's speaking on Sister Eva. Like Miss Soltau herself, that great woman was always ready to re-adjust her vision to a widened horizon, and when she heard of a great door and effectual being opened among the simple aboriginal tribes of West China, she immediately recognized the suitability of her own Deaconesses to take the Gospel to these people.

In 1911 Sister Eva came to England in order to consult with the C.I.M. authorities regarding this plan, and in the following January Miss Soltau had the great joy of welcoming four Friedenshort Deaconesses to her house.

On July 1 of that same year this first party left for China to undertake a service which has been signally owned and blessed of God.

It will be readily understood that the declaration of war between England and Germany was a shattering blow to Miss Soltau's household. The first responsibility of the China Inland Mission was the repatriation of the foreign students, and this had to be done under the most difficult conditions of national suspicion. Inside the house, as throughout the wider organization of the C.I.M., the bond of spiritual union was strong enough to maintain fellowship between men and women who recognized the super-national unity of their one faith.

When the foreign students had left, the British girls began to melt away also, and finally Miss Soltau was left with two students only, both of whom were children of missionaries. It was an anxious time in which to bear the responsibility of even these, but one of them writes of the atmosphere of calm which pervaded the home even during the worst war experiences that London suffered : " Air raids and war uncertainty could not rob Miss Soltau's home of its peace. I had to sit for an exam. in a hall at the top of a large building in the City, during one of the worst of all the London air raids and I thought how anxious Miss Soltau would be. I rushed home to find her serene and calm, quite certain that prayer had been answered for the absent one."

Miss Soltau herself writes : " In view of ever-increasing war cost something must be done to lessen expenses. . . . We have therefore agreed to give up one of the houses in December and empty another of furniture, which will save the rates and taxes. . . . We shall not lose our packing rooms nor all our good store cupboards, where I have so much outfit ready. . . . We shall lose our splendid classrooms where we have held so many large meetings. . . . It is at no small cost that I see the work suddenly, through the War, really taken out of my hands. . . . The Lord, Who has so graciously carried us through these fourteen years in these houses, is with us still, to sustain the work, guide and direct ; we only want His will to be done."

In a private letter, written at the same time, she says : " Don't be troubled about this new plan for our dear home. You will know something must be done in days when every week prices rise. Our Father is surely guiding us step by step. He knows what is before us, we know not. We think we shall only be seven in family after Easter holidays and we have forty-two beds and the same number of chests-of-drawers, washstands and small tables, in the bedrooms. We cannot even keep the place dusted, and we must lessen the expense of char-women. Phil. 4. 19 is ours in war-time, so with joyful heart I say, 'I will fear no evil for Thou art with me.' After all I think I will not entirely empty No. 90, but keep the class-room open for Y.W.C.A., Prayer Circle and Teachers' meetings, or people will think no work is going on and that will not do, so I am hoping for this quarter to pay the rates myself for No. 90 and in June we shall know better what to do. . . . I cannot write more. A very heavy snowstorm since 5 a.m., so cold, and now a dark fog is coming. We have not had such a winter for a quarter of a century. . . . My fur coat is such a comfort. Thank you both for it. I think of you as I put it on. . . . I am so well clothed, I feel sometimes obliged to tell people that the things were given to me."

X

DURING the many years when neither Boxers in China nor war in Europe broke up the routine of the house, the inflow and outflow of candidates went steadily on. One who was there for many years writes as follows :

"Each day started with the ringing of a gong at 6.30 a.m. Prayers were at 8 o'clock, before breakfast. No one could ever induce Miss Soltau to have an early cup of tea ! and she could not bear anyone to enter her room until she had had her quiet time.

"If the student on class-room duty in winter was a good fire-maker there was a feeling of general thanksgiving as we entered ; if not we were enjoined to ' endure hardness.' Miss Soltau certainly never shirked in this direction personally. Her study and bedroom were both on the north side of the house, at the back, chosen partly to avoid the noise of the traffic, but consequently sunless. I remember how really delighted she was when someone taking prayers one day commented on Ezekiel 40. 46: ' The chamber whose prospect is towards the north is for the priests.' She was really in the priestly succession !

"After breakfast she always visited the kitchen,

ordering meals and stores, and at 10 o'clock led
Intercession, reading all the names of the missionaries at their different stations from the Prayer
List; often a Bible Reading to the students followed,
and then she would go to her study and take up her
correspondence, returning again shortly after
the midday dinner till 5 o'clock tea, and yet again
for further work in the evening. Saturday morn-
ings were devoted to accounts, always accurately
kept but entailing a great deal of strain, for she
was not naturally quick at figures. Nor were
meal-times a rest, for she reserved China letters to
read aloud at table.

"It was usually my 'job' to meet foreign
students at the station and pilot them back to the
Training Home, where a very warm welcome
awaited each one from Miss Soltau. But I remember
the arrival one Sunday afternoon of two very young
Norwegians. The one responsible for sending
them unfortunately forgot to advise us of the day
and time of arrival, and they were stranded at the
London station with no one to meet them and
knowing literally not a word of English except
that they were going to the 'Kina Inland Mission.'
We were thankful indeed to the agent of the
National Vigilance Society for taking a taxi and
bringing them safely home.

"These two girls had fresh little faces and fair,
curly hair, which made them look like two very

pretty wax dolls, but like most of the foreigners who came to us they were anything but doll-like in their characters, for having come to help in the kitchen work they turned to with a will, and in less than six months, besides scrubbing tables to an unprecedented state of whiteness, they were speaking English as fluently as some who had been in England for years."

Miss Soltau's wide-flung draw-net sometimes caught queer fish, and it was a discipline to stand by and see her showering kindness on unworthy recipients.

" Among those who took advantage of her goodness were a Jewess and her daughter, who professed conversion and got a glorious holiday in Kent to escape persecution, and a Roman Catholic girl who came over from Ireland to evade the priests, and turned out to be a kleptomaniac ! "

In this connection one who was a candidate in the house writes:

" Being just one girl among the number, I was able to see how some of the students played up to Miss Soltau by emphasizing the points which attracted her most. For this reason, several of whom she thought highly proved a disappointment when they got out to China. One of the number was a regular fraud. She arrived at the house with a marvellous story of Divine interposition on her behalf which, some of us felt, would need corroboration before we could really believe it. Not so Miss Soltau. The candidate was received into special favour which assured her endless privileges. Such marvellous happenings marked every incident of her career that some of us had a great wish to investigate her narrations and unmask her if they should prove false. We felt small when she left for her post abroad (not C.I.M.) still in the odour of sanctity, but two years later Miss Soltau had the grief of knowing that she had proved an utter failure."

The cases in which she was deceived were, however, exceedingly few compared with those she truly helped. She was constantly guided to people in need and enabled to assist them. The witness of one who was in a position to know is : " Considering the vast number of candidates whom she handled it was surprising how few mistakes were made. It was wonderful to observe her gift of meeting the great variety of character and temperament among them. The saving element was that the grace of God in her made her able to recognize the same grace, and the working of the Holy Spirit, in those with whom otherwise she would have had little touch. She was always willing to give unlikely and unpromising candidates the opportunity of proving themselves fit if there seemed to be material that might develop ; and how often her love and patience were rewarded."

Most of the house-work was done by the students. One of them writes : " We had no servants and used to take our turn in the kitchen, two at a time. I was impressed by Miss Soltau's indifference to the food question, and how she cheerfully ate whatever weird dish was produced by the amateur cooks. I often wondered if she thought to test me when I was put in the kitchen with our own parlourmaid, who offered to the C.I.M. shortly after I did. If so it failed, as Ada insisted on doing all the dirty jobs and Miss Lucy had rather a good time."

While the household slept Miss Soltau often prayed. She desired to be alert to the least suggestion of God's Spirit, and often when she awoke in the night she would remember one or another who, later on, she came to know, had been in special need at that time.

One night she was awakened by a pressing call to prayer. She rose, prayed and slept again, but awoke a second time with a strong sense of danger on her. Taking up her Daily Light her eye fell on the verses for the day : " When thou passest through the waters I will be with thee, and through the rivers, they shall not overflow thee." Reading them she became convinced that danger centred round a party of missionaries then in the China Sea. This time she got up and spent a long time in prayer, nor could she desist until she had assurance that their safety was certain. At that very hour the ship was battling in a typhoon and in danger of being swallowed up. When their letters reached her she heard that in anxiety and distress one of the party had called out, " O that Miss Soltau might know our danger and pray for us ! "

The ship and all on board came safely to port.

XI

ONE of the petitions most frequently heard on the lips of Henrietta Soltau when in prayer, was that from her, or from those for whom she was praying, or from the household of which she stood as head, there might flow life-streams to the uttermost parts of the earth. Among the notes and diary records of the addresses and Bible Readings which she gave so frequently, and in so many places, we constantly read this sentence, " My subject was the River of Life." It is evident that, of the various similies used by the writers of the Old and New Testaments, none seemed to her so perfect an illustration of the Spirit of God, filling and controlling believing souls.

Time, as money, was to her a sacred trust intended to be spent unstintingly upon those who were needing it. She was nearly always to be found in her house, and though no one ever found her idle those who had need of her found her leisured. She was always at home, in every sense of the word, to those who made a legitimate claim upon her. The missionary on furlough, whether eager to relate some encouraging aspect of her work, or burdened with a sense of failure, the factory girl clamouring for a hearing of her wrongs, the minister asking for spiritual help, the poor lady seeking to sell some heirloom in order to supply herself with bare necessities, the prospective missionary candidate discouraged by the refusal of more than one society, the homeless foreigner stranded friendless in London, all these instinctively turned to her for help, nor were they disappointed.

To record one instance taken from a private letter : " Three days ago I had a visit from a Minister of this neighbourhood. Those who attended his church had often said how little help they were getting from his ministry. He seemed to be a good man, but burdened his sermons with reference to controversial matter. How little they knew through what a conflict he was passing. I was amazed to see him enter my study and to hear him say in his impulsive way : ' You are a good woman, Miss Soltau, and I have come to you for help.' For an hour we talked solely of spiritual matters, and he told me of his lonely conflicts and struggles as he faced his congregation each Sunday. ' How can I preach to them when my own heart is so tumultuous and unsatisfied ? ' I endeavoured to share with him my own experience, and the certainty of victory which comes with the indwelling of the Holy Spirit.

" The following Sunday I was much in prayer for him and I attended morning service at his church. He saw me, and as he entered the pulpit he turned and gave me an understanding look. He preached with power, and that day more than one remarked on the change both in his bearing and message. The solemnity of the Communion Service on that Sunday morning I can never forget. I heard no more of him until Tuesday afternoon when a caller asked me if I had heard of his sudden death from heart failure but a few hours previously. I felt deeply humbled as I thought how little I had been able to help him; now he is satisfied."

By correspondence she kept in close touch with nearly all those who had passed through her house and were missionaries in China, and also with hundreds who, for one reason or another, had been refused for missionary work by the C.I.M. Always on the alert for anything which might prove of spiritual uplift to lonely people on the Mission field she made it a habit to take careful notes of sermons and conference addresses which impressed her. Of these notes the following reproduced from a private letter written to the authors when she was in her eightieth year, will serve as an example. They show the clearness of her longhand notes, and the accuracy of her thought:

"I want to tell you about the Good Friday service at Regent Square Presbyterian Church and of the beautiful sermon preached that day by Dr. Ivor Roberton, for I know what an inspiration his ministry was to you during your last furlough.

It was a most sacred and solemn time. The hymns were beautifully chosen and twice sufficient time was allowed for silent prayer, during which the hush of God's presence was manifest.

" The subject of the sermon was ' The Five Great Sins which characterised those who crucified Christ.'

" First. The expediency of Caiaphas. John 18. 14.

" He did not say, ' It is right that one should die for the people ' but, ' It is expedient.' He dared not say, ' It would be doing right to put him to death.'

" How many even of God's own children do things from expediency and thus crucify afresh the Son of God.

" Secondly. The determined injustice of Pilate. John 18. 38 and 19. 4–6.

" Three times he had proved Him guiltless. ' I find in him no fault at all.'

" Yet he scourged Him, delivered Him to the soldiery, delivered Him to be crucified.

" Had he set Him free, what would have happened? Maybe he would have lost his post as Governor, but he would have found his Saviour.

" Thirdly. The brutal cruelty and ribaldry of the Roman soldiers. John 19. 2, 3.

" The Son of God handed over to them. Crowned with thorns, mocked, smitten by their cruel hands, robed in purple, spat upon, knees bowed in mockery.

" Why did He suffer thus ? He loved us and gave Himself for us.

" Fourthly. The treachery of Judas. Luke 22. 47, 48.

" Alas, there are those who still kiss but to betray. How astonished Judas must have been when the Lord said to him, ' Judas, betrayest thou the Son of man with a kiss ? '

" Christ reads the motives of the heart. He sees the treachery, we may only feel the kiss.

" Fifthly. The cowardice of His disciples. Matt. 26. 56.

" ' They all forsook Him and fled.' What ! Peter ? John ? Yea, none stood by Him in that awful hour of betrayal.

" Do we fear to confess our Blessed Lord ? How often we too have failed.

" How did Christ meet the sins of Judas, Pilate, the ruffian soldiers, the fearful disciples ? He flung the light of truth upon their sin.

" Judas convicted by His Words who read his heart.

" Pilate compelled to ask, ' What is Truth ? '

" The centurion saved as he gazed on the dying Lamb of God.

" The disciples restored and renewed when He appeared to them on Easter morning.

" He flung the light of truth on them all.

" Did He call for angelic hosts and destroy His murderers ?   No.

" He accepted the cup from His Father's hand. He drank it to the dregs.

" He took the way of the cross, to be the sin-bearer and the deliverer from sin.

" He rose triumphant to make us more than conquerors through Him that loved us."

" This, darling, is just an imperfect sketch of a message which I trust I shall never forget."

STEADY UNTIL THE GOING DOWN OF THE SUN

I

IN 1919, when England began to emerge from war chaos, Miss Soltau was seventy-six years of age and it was obvious that she could no longer train women for the Mission field. The post-war girl was a different proposition from anything she had previously handled and the too great disparity of age between the students and herself would have been as a chasm across which each might view the other, but at a distance and in a baffled and uncertain mood.

Nor was there any younger woman working with her who could help her through the difficult transitional period, and she now paid the price of her outstanding individualism. There were a number who had helped her for longer or shorter periods, but, strange to relate, not one of them had ever found herself able to fill the post to her own satisfaction. Indeed it has been written: "It is always a sorrowful thought to me that they all left with a sense of disappointment that they had failed, or thought they had failed, to help her in the work as they had wished to do. I think it arose from a lack of making those working for or with her, feel that they were really *fellow*-workers."

Henrietta Soltau had never done team work and did not understand team work. On the few occasions when she met in conference with other women who were engaged in the same kind of service as herself, she appeared in their midst radiant with peace and joy, full of love and kindness, a veritable benediction to the gathering, perhaps the most humble of them all, and yet it never for one moment occurred to her that she could learn anything from them, nor did she.

The choice of the China Inland Mission Council, in appointing her successor, fell on Miss Edith Smith, a missionary who had been compelled to leave China for family reasons, and in this choice Miss Soltau entirely concurred. Before taking over her duties Miss Smith went on a visit to China in order that she might see the more up-to-date conditions of that changeful land. If the young people of England presented problems, those of China were doing so no less, and during the months she spent there, she was busy taking impressions and gleaning information which would help her in the task which lay ahead.

The last two students who were trained in Miss Soltau's hands travelled out to China with Miss Smith under war conditions. After they left there was a pause in the activities of the Women's Home Training Department, and for a time no new applicants were admitted.

The two vacant houses 90 and 92 Grosvenor Road were easily disposed of, for the Mildmay Deaconess Home was being moved from the Conference premises and the houses were taken for their use. Henrietta and Elsie Soltau lived together in 94 Grosvenor Road, which was Henrietta's own house, and when Miss Edith Smith returned from China new premises were bought in Aberdeen Park, where, during May, 1919, a fresh band of candidates commenced their training under her direction.

The next few months were, to Miss Soltau, a period of mental pain. As she saw the work on which she had concentrated all her powers removed from her and given to another, she became victim of the most lacerating self-reproach. She wept many bitter tears and endured endless questionings as to whether everything had been taken from her because of unfaithfulness on her part. For a time nothing availed to comfort her, and only gradually did she regain her calm. The years of war told too heavily upon her and she had carried the burdens and sorrows of too many lives on her own heart. Where she could bring comfort she had never spared herself, and beyond this had spent long hours in prayer for those who needed the consolation which God alone could give.

Miss Soltau now had to learn as a fresh lesson,

the art of living a private life uncontrolled by
gongs, bells, rigid punctuality and the habit of
always weighing her actions in view of being an
example to others. This lesson she learned
admirably and shone afresh with a long-retarded
afterglow, amazing her intimates by her adaptability to new conditions and her interest in the
changing trend of modern life.

Formerly her own scrupulous care lest she
cause others to stumble had reacted on her
friends, who were wont to spare her so much
as a reference to things of which she would
certainly disapprove. Gradually this all changed
and they found her ready to be genuinely interested, even where she could not agree.

She had no intention of settling down to the
life of an old lady until she was obliged to do
so. She even took speaking engagements and,
when she was eighty years old, addressed a
large audience for forty minutes on missionary
work in China. She still personally handled
the correspondence, the accounts and the distribution of goods which reached her from the
Helping Hands Association, and always attended
the Women's Council meetings of which she
was made Chairman.

II

ALL through her long life Henrietta Soltau had been a bearer of responsibilities. The care of her blind father, the charge of the missionaries' children, the training of the missionary candidates, and finally the responsibility of her sister Elsie, whose delicacy was complicated by almost total blindness. These were some of the burdens that she had borne.

For thirteen years the two sisters lived together at 94 Grosvenor Road, a house unnecessarily large and expensive to run, but one to which Elsie Soltau clung. At her sister's death Henrietta was released from this final claim and for the first time in her life, at the age of eighty-five, was able to choose her own mode of life in accordance with her own personal tastes, and without the need of putting someone else's demands before her own.

She knew quite well what she wanted: a small, sunny, airy flat, and above all things a garden. It must be in North London, for she could not think of being far from the headquarters of the C.I.M. She did not require to search for the premises she needed, for on the very day of Elsie's funeral a friend brought her

news which made her next step clear. Alterations were being made at the Egypt General
Mission house, Highbury New Park, and a self-
contained garden flat would be to let. That very
day the rooms were inspected and found to be
suitable in every respect. Her cousin, Miss
Edith Bewes, writes : " It was the very thing
needed by Miss Soltau. The E.G.M. altered it
and we moved in. Even the way into the
garden was stairless, and how she loved that
garden ! She sat out whenever it was possible,
and had her meals served to her on the lawn.
She would walk among the flower beds, leaning
on a companion's arm, and delighting to watch
the different plants grow and flower."

Miss Soltau herself wrote : " I can only praise
the Lord for giving me such a sweet resting place.
It is so beautifully done up and arranged. There
is a large sitting-room which holds all my old
drawing-room furniture and a small dining-table.
My pictures are going up, and my study set of the
Tabernacle pictures. There are three nice bedrooms, cosy and comfortable, a kitchen and good
larder, so that we have everything we need including a bathroom. . . . We do not notice
the noise at all from the road and the back is
perfectly quiet by night. You see how compassed we are with loving kindness and tender
mercies.

"Dear Eva McCarthy has been my good helper in the move. She had an amusing time with the electricians who were slow in getting on with the work, so one day she sat in the office for two hours and refused to budge until she got them to come and finish the job.

"I have been giving away plants from the garden at 94 Grosvenor Road. I have already disposed of a quantity of our lilies of the valley which did so well that Miss Bewes picked 852 blooms from our bed last spring."

During the years that followed she remained practically without other illness than that caused by the weakness of her heart. Her needs were few, but chief among them was the necessity of a nurse who, if she were ill or Miss Bewes had to leave her, could come and take charge. Another was that of a reliable young woman to handle the domestic work. Both of these were supplied in the persons of two sisters, Edith and Annie Larby, whose loving service was one of the joys of her last years. The two girls had been left orphans very young and had been brought up in the homes of George Müller, at Bristol. On Miss Soltau's death Edith Larby wrote: "How we shall all miss the dear one and how wonderful it is to Annie and myself that we two poor orphans should have been allowed to serve this saint of God."

It was one of her hopes that she might live long enough to see again those whom she affectionately called her 'beloved Trio,' and their little Topsy. This desire was granted and no one who saw it will ever forget the snow-haired, ethereal saint, clasping the sturdy little Mongolian in her arms.

A last New Year entry in her diary runs: January 1, 1933. "Loving kindness and tender mercies as I enter this New Year. How much I have to praise my Lord for. Psalm 103."

In the same year, under November 14, she wrote: "Dear Francesca paid me a visit this morning. She so kindly brought me some grapes. Mildred and Eva taking Topsy to Miss Wheeler (at the school for deaf mutes) where she will spend the day. Edith later read me the interesting book *Forty Remarkable People*. It was Dr. Barnardo's life to-night. Nurse kindly helped me to bed."

These were the last words she wrote. Immediately after she had a seizure which left her right arm helpless, and she was carried over to 77, Highbury New Park, where in the beautiful Nursing Home of the China Inland Mission, she had for the last few weeks of her life, the personal care of her loving friend Mary Taylor, Superintendent of the home.

December 8, 1933, was her ninetieth birthday.

She lay propped by pillows in a room which was a bower of flowers. Her hair was like snow, her eyes blue as forget-me-nots, and there were delicate pink touches to her pillow and shawl. With joy she fingered the numerous letters which brought her messages of love from all quarters of the globe, and when the short winter day was drawing to a close, a few intimates knelt in her room at a celebration of the Holy Communion.

That day she was radiantly happy, satisfied with long life and her eyes fixed on the pleasures which awaited her at God's right hand. She lingered until February 5, 1934, often very weary, yet sometimes able to enjoy the reading aloud of certain books.

Increasingly she lived in the past and the future. One of her visitors, finding her sunk in lethargy and desiring to call her attention, sat down by her, saying :

" Miss Soltau, do you remember Miss S. in Devonshire ? "

Consciousness re-animated her face, and quite alertly she said, " Yes, my dear, I do, and I well remember her mother who came to Barnstaple when I was a child."

Then she talked on for a long time, moving among past scenes and speaking of those who were dead. At last she referred to her own conversion eighty years before.

"There have been no wasted years for you to lament, Miss Soltau."

"No, my dear," she said strongly, "no wasted years, no wasted years."

Her illness was long enough for news to reach even the most remote of her scattered and incalculably large spiritual family, and "the road was full of people waiting to see her take her journey."

The next time her friends gathered together was on February 8, and it was for her funeral. None dared to mourn. The grave is in Finchley Cemetery.

She was sustained to the last with every needful comfort, but she had no worldly goods to dispose of, and her legacies were in the realm of the spirit. She wrote in her Will:

"It is impossible to mention all the beloved friends who have been so closely linked with me for so many years in joys and sorrows in the homeland and in China. I send them all my deep love and gratitude for all their sustainment in prayers, and in love and gifts.

". . . To my large missionary family I send my deep love. Tell them to stand fast and be faithful 'till He come.' We only say 'Good night.' We meet at Dawn of Day. May each one run with patience the race set before her, 'looking off unto Jesus.'"

"Soon they will come rejoicing, bringing in the sheaves. . . .   The Eternal Bonds—how unspeakably precious to us, and all coming through the free grace of God, the Father of our Lord Jesus Christ, Who has redeemed us with His precious blood, His love revealed to us by the Blessed Comforter.

> 'I stand upon His merit,
> I know no other stand,
> Not e'en where glory dwelleth,
> In Immanuel's land.'

"With deep love.   A sinner saved by grace.
        "HENRIETTA ELIZA SOLTAU."

EPILOGUE

"I SEE myself now at the end of my journey, my toilsome days are ended. I am going now to see that head that was crowned with thorns and that face that was spit upon for me. I have formerly lived by hearsay and faith; but now I go where I shall live by sight and shall be with Him in whose company I delight myself. I have loved to hear my Lord spoken of; and wherever I have seen the print of His shoe in the earth there I have coveted to set my foot too. His name has been to me as a civet box; yea, sweeter than all perfume. His voice to me has been most sweet; and his countenance I have more desired than they that have most desired the light of the sun. His word I did use to gather for my food, and for antidotes against my faintings. He has held me, and I have kept me from mine iniquities; yea, my steps hath He strengthened in His way."

The Young Woman
who Lived in a Shoe

For the past 20 years Elizabeth Braund has been working with young people in inner city London. Her attempts to start a youth club in an old disused Battersea Baptist chapel led to the foundation of Providence House.

The 'Young Woman who Lived in a Shoe' describes how she overcame her own misgivings and doubts, and persuaded the local and church authorities through her unique work, that youngsters who are 'Street wise' can also become 'Society wise'.

Elizabeth Braund's intuitive grasp of complex situations, together with her refusal to accept evangelical clichés or traditional methods greatly contributed to her success. She was able as a result to identify with the people who lived round about her, as they experienced social and spiritual renwal in a tough, inner city neighbourhood.